Between the Lines

Henry Bascom Smith

Between the Lines

Experiences in the Federal Secret Service
during the American Civil War

Henry Bascom-Smith

LEONAUR

Between the Lines
Experiences in the Federal Secret Service
during the American Civil War
by Henry Bascom-Smith

First published under the title
Between the Lines
Secret Service Storiesr

Leonaur is an imprint
of Oakpast Ltd

ISBN: 978-1-84677-884-1 (hardcover)
ISBN: 978-1-84677-883-4 (softcover)

http://www.leonaur.com

Publisher's Notes

In the interests of authenticity, the spellings, grammar and place names
used have been retained from the original editions.

The opinions of the authors represent a view of events in which he
was a participant related from his own perspective,
as such the text is relevant as an historical document.

The views expressed in this book are not necessarily
those of the publisher.

Contents

DEDICATED TO SAMUEL GRAHAM BOOZ
TO WHOSE PERSISTENCY
IN THUMPING OUT ON HIS TYPEWRITER
THE WORDS HEREIN
HAS RENDERED IT POSSIBLE FOR ME
TO INFLICT MY FIFTY-YEAR-OLD STORIES
ON MY FRIENDS

Apology

Fifty years ago! Gracious me! It makes me think of my age to talk of it. Yes, just fifty years ago was enacted the greatest tragedy the world ever saw, *The Civil War*.

I entered the service at twenty and one-half years of age and served three and one-half years.

At different times I have told of some of my experiences, which seemed to interest. Sometimes I have talked to literary men, story writers, who have expressed a desire to write me up in magazines and newspapers, but lack of the romantic in my makeup, notwithstanding romance might be seen in the stories which to me were but cold facts, has kept me from consenting.

I am actuated now by other reasons. I have a lot of documents and memoranda that are wearing out, liable to be mislaid or lost. In fact I have already lost one document, a letter from General Lew Wallace, a very valuable and important one (to me); it was his letter of presentation to me of the Harry Gilmor sword, written on the eve of his departure for Texas (on a secret mission, known only to Lincoln and Grant), to receive the capitulation of the Confederate General Slaughter, hence I feel that these matters ought to be recorded somewhere.

The New York Historical Society and Columbia University have offered some of these documents place in their archives. The affidavit and signature of Paine, the Conspirator who attempted to assassinate Secretary Seward, ought to be in some substantial depository as a link in history. I presume it is the only finger mark extant of any of the conspirators. The reason why I have not deposited it is that the statement appears garbled, requiring me to explain the gaps and hidden meanings between the lines, which I shall try to do in these pages.

Another motive for putting these experiences in writing, is in the interest of Graham, and his children, Curtis, Evelyn and her children,

Nettie and DeLos. It is to be expected these younger ones will remain longer here under the old Flag, and perhaps they may get some consolation from the fact that some of their ancestors did something in simple patriotism. Nettie has complained that her school history did not mention her uncle. I told her I could only be found by reading "between the lines," because there were so many "pebbles on the beach" besides her uncle.

But how can I make it interesting? I am afraid I shall injure the facts in trying to write them. A story writer might make a romance out of almost any one of my stories, for he would dress it up so. Every day and hour of my Secret Service experience was crowded with events; they came swift one after another; for instance the Election Fraud case of 1864 to which *Appleton's Encyclopaedia* devotes columns, took less than five days to develop; the story would take nearly as long to tell.

The Harry Gilmor Sword

The sword of Harry Gilmor, the Confederate colonel, which General Wallace had given me, had aroused Graham's interest so much that I presented it to him; I had, prior to this, presented to Curtis, my Creedmoor rifle trophies. I had become tired of telling the history of that sword and how it came into my possession, having no other evidence than my word for the truth of the story, since I had lost General Wallace's letter. However, quite unexpectedly, the story was revived in the following manner:

Evelyn, who was but a baby in those days, remembering that I was with General Wallace, on Christmas day, 1908, presented me with his *Autobiography* (two volumes) much to my delight. A few days later Aunt Mag, glancing through the second volume, discovered that I was remembered by the General and the sword incident was there officially described, so that now the sword is really vouched for in history, for Wallace's volumes will be in every important library in the world.

I quote from *General Lew Wallace's Autobiography*, page 687 and on:

From what has been said, it would seem my friend, General Schenck, had found a disturbing element in the Secession ladies of Baltimore, and in some way suffered from it. His description of them, and the emphasis with which he had dwelt upon their remarkable talent for mischief in general, I accepted as a warning, and stood upon my guard.

Everyone into whose hands these memoirs may fall will see almost of his own suggestion how necessary it was that, of the inhabitants of the city, I should know who were disloyal with more certainty even than who were loyal; of the latter there was nothing to fear, while of the former there was at least eve-

11

rything to suspect. We knew communication with the enemy across the line was unceasing; that interchange of news between Richmond and Baltimore was of daily occurrence; that there were routes, invisible to us, by which traffic in articles contraband of war was carried on with singular success, almost as a legitimate commerce—routes by water as well as by land. General Butler, at Norfolk, exerted himself to discover the traders operating by way of the Chesapeake Bay, but without success; with a like result I tried to unearth the landward lines.

Captain Smith, my chief of detectives, a man of ability and zeal, at last brought me proof incontestable that Baltimore was but a wayside station of the nefarious commerce, the initial points of active transaction centring in Philadelphia.

As to Baltimore, this simplified our task, and shortly General Schenck's sagacity was again vindicated—those working in the prohibited business were ladies who moved in the upper circles of society.

Should I arrest the fair sympathizers? What was the use? The simple appearance of distress was enough with the President; and if that were so with a man in concernment, what would it be with a woman? In sight of the hopelessness of effort on my part, over and over, again and again, in the night often as in the day, I took counsel of myself, 'What can be done?' At last an answer came to me, and in a way no one could have dreamed—the purest chance.

A woman in high standing socially, alighted from a carriage at the Camden station of the Baltimore and Ohio Railroad, carrying a mysterious-looking box. At the moment she was stepping into a car my chief of detectives arrested her. The box being opened, there, in velvet housings, lay a sword of costly pattern inscribed for presentation to Colonel ——, a guerilla officer of Confederate renown.

A commission was immediately ordered for the woman's trial. The word and the inscription upon it were irrefutable proofs of guilt, and she was sent to a prison for females in Massachusetts. The affair was inexcusably gross, considering the condition of war—so much, I think, will be generally conceded—still, seeking the moral effect of punishment alone, I specially requested the officials of the institution not to subject the offender to humiliation beyond the mere imprisonment. In a few days she was released and brought home. *The sword I presented to Captain Smith.*

General Wallace makes a slight error. I did not arrest the woman at the station, but captured her messenger with the sword, and upon his person were credentials to Gilmor, which I used myself, and of which I will tell later on. Later on I arrested the woman herself.

Aunt Mag

During the first year of the war ('61) I remained at home, but I was really ashamed to be found there when service called. Burdette was already in the Army, and A. P., though equally patriotic, was compelled to remain home to "fight for bread" for the family. I started to go but mother restrained me; finally, however, Olive persuaded mother to consent, and on January 10th, 1862, I began my service as 2nd lieutenant in the 5th N.Y. Heavy Artillery. In the early part of '62 our Regiment garrisoned the forts of New York Harbor. I was stationed first at Fort Wood (Bedloe's Island), and afterwards at Fort Schuyler, where I was Post Adjutant.

Fort Schuyler is a very extensive fortification guarding the entrance to New York from the east, situated on a peninsula called Throggs Neck, where there is an abrupt turn from the waters of the East River as it enters Long Island Sound; the channel is quite narrow at that point. The fortification comprises two tiers of casemates surmounted by a parapet, and on the landward side barbette batteries. A first-class formidable defence for the arms of those days. The interior of Fort Schuyler was large enough to enable a battalion to form in line. At that time there was under construction on the opposite, or Long Island, shore, on Willet's Point, a fortification which has since been completed and is called Fort Totten.

In May, '62, we were withdrawn from the forts in New York Harbor. We were ordered to the front, to join the army at Fortress Monroe, Virginia. We were assembled, taken by steamers to Amboy, thence by the old Camden and Amboy Railroad to Camden and Philadelphia, thence by the Philadelphia, Wilmington and Baltimore Railroad to Baltimore. We were handsomely treated to a meal in the "Soldiers' Rest" in Philadelphia, by the patriotic ladies. God bless them! We were transported in box freight cars, rough board benches for seats. No drawing-room cars in those days.

On arriving in Baltimore we were loaded upon a steamer for Fortress Monroe. At this point our orders were changed. Being a heavy artillery regiment, we were ordered to garrison Fort Marshal (near Baltimore), relieving the 3rd Delaware, an infantry regiment. We were marched through the city to Fort Marshal. Later we learned that the Baltimoreans dubbed us the "toughest" they had seen. Our appearance was misleading, we thought.

Fort Marshal was an earth work, a parapet with bastions, erected on an eminence just east of Baltimore, commanding the harbour and the city. It has since been demolished, crowded out by commerce and residences.

When we arrived at the fort our men were hungry, having had but "one square meal" in forty-eight hours—the one the Philadelphia ladies had given us, plus what was picked up from pie peddlers on the way. We learned the lesson all green troops must learn, when inefficiency of the commissary is shown. I volunteered to get feed for the men; the Colonel accepted my tender. I went down to the city limits, pressed three wagons (those deep box-wagons in use in Baltimore) into service, drove to the Quartermaster's Department in South Gay Street, represented myself as Acting Quartermaster (which was a little out of "plumb" but excusable by the emergency) and drew three wagon loads of aerated bread and coffee, drove back to camp, turned the kettles up and had the men banqueting inside of two hours. Inefficiency was surely our Commissary's right name.

At this point I want to tell something about Aunt Mag, my "Star in the East," who has ever since guided me.

Union people and the Star Spangled Banner were not so plenty in Maryland. Not far from Fort Marshal I espied a cheerful looking house. In its yard from a flagstaff was unfurled our glorious emblem. That was the house of Aunt Mag. I fell in love with the premises, and very soon with its occupant. Later on I was stricken down with that dreadful army plague, typhoid fever, and I was very near to death. That house was my hospital, and Aunt Mag was my nurse. I lived, and so here we are after fifty years. Many friends have remarked, how romantic! but we say it is just love. If the "Over-ruling Hand" was not in it, it certainly has proven a fortunate "happen so" for our lives have so nicely matched in the "pinions" as to have needed no other lubrication than love for all these years.

The house referred to was the home of Thomas Booz (the father of Graham and Curtis). He was a real "19th of April" Union man; and on that eventful day he defended his premises with a gun. He was of the firm of Thos. Booz & Brother, shipbuilders; also he was a member of the Legislature, and was talked of for Governor. Their firm built the pontoons that McClellan used to recross the Potomac at Harper's Ferry in 1862, after Antietam; they also built one of the first turreted monitors (the Waxsaw), patterned after Ericsson's Monitor which fought the battle with the Merrimac.

What do I mean by an "April 19th" Union man? Well, I will tell you: On that day was shed the first blood of the war. A mob attacked the 6th Massachusetts Regiment in Pratt Street, as it was proceeding to Washington (April 19th, 1861). Like magic all Marylanders took sides, one part for the Union, the other for Rebellion. Ever after the prime question or test of loyalty was, how did you stand on April 19th? A Union man on that day was ever after one. Families were divided. It cost a deal to be a Union man there or in any of the border States. I have often thought they deserved as much consideration as those who fought battles.

In August, 1862, two companies, A and F, of our Regiment were detailed to go to Harper's Ferry to man batteries there. There being a vacancy in the line (in Co. A) I requested to be detailed to it, but my superior objected, claiming I was necessary with my own company. I was not permitted to go. Had I gone I would have been in that fight and would have been in the Colonel Miles surrender, along with Joe Barker and the rest. Joe's story of spiking the guns of The Naval Battery on Maryland Heights, preparatory to surrender was always interesting. His story of the four days' fighting, sustained as it is by Confederate documents, makes new history. He makes it quite plain that the detention of the enemy there saved us Antietam and perhaps Washington.

The Monitor "Waxsaw"

Trip to Johnson's Island

In the winter of '62-'63 our Regiment was removed to Fort McHenry, where Confederate prisoners of war were detained. General W. W. Morris, an old regular, commanded the Brigade (Headquarters were there) and Colonel Peter A. Porter (whose monument is at Goat Island, Niagara Falls) commanded the Post. We were carrying there about one thousand Confederate and political prisoners. A large percentage of them were commissioned officers.

Early in '63 our Regiment was ordered to the front by way of Harper's Ferry. When we arrived at the Ferry I was the first officer detailed for a two-days' turn of picket duty on Bolivar Heights.

Harper's Ferry is situated at the confluence of the Potomac and Shenandoah rivers. The Potomac cuts through the Blue Ridge Mountains there. The Chesapeake and Ohio Canal runs along the north bank of the Potomac, rugged mountains enclose it, presenting an alpine appearance. Here the "John Brown raid" began. It was formerly the location of one of the great national arsenals. When encamped there in '63 the Regiment was in tents on Camp Hill; the officers were quartered in a building which had been the home of the officers of the arsenal.

Our Regiment, nominally a heavy artillery regiment, was thoroughly schooled in the heavy tactics and also as light or field artillery and infantry; able or qualified to be used in either arm of the service with equal facility. The order to proceed to the front was hailed with delight, duty in the field being a panacea for garrison bickerings.

Later the regiment was moved to Halltown, encamped on the Miller farm, and threw out pickets. I was on first detail there. I learned how to get a fair sleep on top of a "herring-bone" rail fence. My proclivity for "prying into things" manifested itself there. An attack was

LIEUTENANT JOSEPH H. (JOE) BARKER

expected, so our regiment slept on arms, anxiously waiting; it became tedious. I asked permission to reconnoitre alone, and was permitted. In the dark I sneaked out about a mile, and listened; three or four cavalrymen came whirling down the road as if riding for life; they roused the regiment. They were blood stained, but upon examination the blood was found to have come from one of their own horses. Such scares and mistakes were frequent, especially with fresh troops. I was in a dilemma to get back into line without being shot, but it was accomplished. The regiment was ordered back to Baltimore for garrison duty.

I was detailed to convey prisoners away many times. Once I took ninety odd Confederate officers to Johnson's Island, Sandusky, Ohio. Among them was Lieutenant General Pemberton, who had commanded at Vicksburg, and who had, on July 4th, surrendered Vicksburg with thirty-seven thousand men, fifteen general officers and sixty thousand stand of arms. I was surprised at the great number of "Copperheads" we met in crossing Ohio. My exhibition of Confederate prisoners was treated as a first-class circus; it "drew" the "Copperheads" and they flocked to the stations along the route to express sympathy and admiration.

What was a "Copperhead"? I will try to tell you: he stood, relatively, as the Tories to the Revolution. They were composed of several elements; some were so greedy of gain they wanted no war that might interfere with their finances; some were too cowardly; some were too partisan politically, really thinking their fealty was due to those who were fighting against an administration nominally representing an opposing political party; all of them forming a mass to be influenced by conspirators who were pursuing an intelligent purpose to destroy the Union; just such material as was needed by Vallandigham, Seymour, Andrews, Morgan and Lee to help their projects of further disruption. What became of them? They sank out of sight when the Confederate cause was lost. Naturally they were scorned by the men who had fought for the Union. As time goes on, they and their work is being forgotten. Future historians may be more kind to them than we who suffered because of them, but it is not likely that the descendants of any Copperhead will claim public honours for their anti-Union forbears.

I am reminded of an incident that was told widely through the armies: When Lee's army reached York, Pa., on the way to Gettysburg, these Copperheads went out to meet the Confederates, and assure them "how they had always loved them." The Confederates wanted tangible proof of this love; they demanded that one hundred thousand dollars in gold be paid at once; else the town of York would be burned. Now, wasn't that unkind! but lovers must ever be ready to prove, you know.

On our way home we had a railroad smash at Mifflin, Pa. I was curled up, asleep in my seat, but received only a scratch on my forehead. I crawled out of a window and helped recover bodies from the wreckage.

Fort McHenry is an historic spot. The scene described in our "Star Spangled Banner" was dedicated to it. It was its ramparts Key referred to in his first verse. In 1812 the fort was garrisoned by one thousand men under Major Armisted, to guard Baltimore from an attack by sea. September 13th, 1814, the British admiral, with sixteen heavy war vessels, opened bombardment upon the fort. Its guns failed to reach the fleet till some of the vessels approached nearer. He met so warm a reception that they withdrew, badly damaged. A force of one thousand men landed to surprise the fort in the rear, but they were repulsed. At midnight the firing ceased. Next day the fleet withdrew and Baltimore was safe. During the bombardment Francis Scott Key, a prisoner on board the British fleet, wrote the *Star Spangled Banner*.

I shall never forget July 4th, 1863. The crucial battle of the war, Gettysburg, was being fought. Meade had just succeeded Hooker in command of the army. Anxiously the wisdom of the change was being watched by every soldier. It was my fortune to be detailed as officer of the guard at Fort McHenry that day. Guardmount is always an inspiring exercise, for then troops are carefully inspected and instructed before entry on their tour of duty. Fort McHenry is an ideally beautiful spot, situated on the point of a peninsula formed by the confluence of the north and south forks of the Patapsco River. The spot is loved by every American. A picture, a combination of events, produced the most strikingly emotional effect upon me. We were formed on the exact ground overlooked by Key when he wrote:

Oh, say, can you see, by the dawn's early light,
What so proudly we hailed at the twilight's last gleaming,
Whose broad stripes and bright stars, thro' the perilous fight,
O'er the ramparts we watched, were so gallantly streaming?
And the rockets' red glare, the bombs bursting in air,
Gave proof thro' the night that our flag was still there.
Oh, say, does that star spangled banner yet wave,

21

O'er the land of the free and the home of the brave?

I was trying to examine arms. Our Post Band, the 2nd Artillery Band, one of the grandest in the service, was playing that soul lifting piece. The north fork of the Patapsco was filled with transports, carrying bronzed veterans (I think the 19th Corps), who were hurrying to Gettysburg, and these boys were yelling for twice their number; cheers upon cheers. On the balcony of one of our prison buildings was a prisoner of war, a lineal descendant of Francis Scott Key, overlooking the scene. And I thought of our flag over yonder to the northwest, forty miles away at Gettysburg. Yesterday and day before we had listened, straining our ears to hear the guns. Was our flag still there? Had our boys with Meade stood fast against the lion of the Confederacy, or had the Stars and Bars been flaunted victorious upon the battle ground?

God knows how our hearts were strained in those hours. And when I heard the cheers of our soldiers upon the transports and thought of Francis Scott Key and how he had watched to see if Old Glory still waved, my eyes were blinded with tears. I had to suspend my inspection to dry them. I was not alone affected; there were many. Such tears one need not be ashamed of; they are not evidence of weakness. An army of men inspired by such emotions would be best to avoid.

I shall never forget the relief which came to our anxiety the next morning (July 5th), Gettysburg was ours. Lee was started back to Virginia. Vicksburg, too, was ours. Indeed, crucial was the day, July 4th, 1863. Every one of our ninety millions of united Americans should ever give thanks for the events of that day.

The Laurel Incident

I had a little taste of the draft riots during that memorable week beginning July 13th, 1863. I was ordered to David's Island, New York Harbor, with seven hundred wounded Confederates from Gettysburg. The demonstrations of the mob of onlookers in Philadelphia were so very unfriendly that we had to use the butts of our muskets to control the crowd. They threatened us saying, "tomorrow will be our day." I understood the threat when I learned later of the rioting. We were advised that our train was to be intercepted before reaching New York, and transportation was, therefore, furnished on the steamer *Commodore*, by the outside course.

After leaving our prisoners at David's Island, we landed at the Battery, and there I addressed my men, cautioning them not to reply to any assault unless ordered by me. We marched up Broadway to the City Hall Barracks (where the New York Post Office now stands) and stacked arms inside the enclosure. I was proud of my men. Each one appeared a giant, steady, firm of step, lips compressed; two-thirds of them were foreign born, yet no better Americans ever paraded Broadway.

Immediately after stacking arms, a lot of rioters who had just overcome their guards, seized our stacks. Our boys jumped on them and I had a big job to keep them from crushing their ribs. Exceeding my orders, I permitted my men to visit their homes, to report back at midnight. The cars were running but had no passengers. I rode on the Eighth Avenue car to 48th Street, my home. Our house was locked, but Cousin Wilbur F. Strong was there alone. He said Brother A. P. had taken the family into the country for safety. A. P.'s loyalty had made him a "marked man," and he had been threatened. After eating, Wilbur and I walked down to John Hardy's, in 35th Street. Stores were all closed, no one on the streets but an occasional corner loafer, who snarled at us. Hardy had been hiding his coloured servant in the coal cellar, to save her life. Wilbur afterwards entered the service, and went on the "Hunter raid" up the Shenandoah Valley in 1864. He died from the exhaustion of the marches.

At midnight every man was behind his stacked arms, ready for duty. The city was deserted, as if plague stricken. I shall never forget the desolation.

Ostensibly the draft was the excuse, but with the moving spirits it was but a subterfuge. The ringleader of the mobs in New York was a mysterious stranger, a "Mr. Andrews" of Virginia. On July 13th, 1863, at 40th Street and Fourth Avenue, while the firemen were at work in Third Avenue, he ascended a shanty which stood opposite the burning ruins. Thousands were assembled behind this shanty in an open space of untilled ground, and the Virginian orator proceeded to address them. He cried out that he wished he had the lungs of a stentor and that there was a reporter present to take down his words; he said he had lately addressed them in Cooper Institute, where he told them Mr. Lincoln wanted to tear the hardworking man from his wife and family and send him to the war; he denounced Mr. Lincoln for his conscription bill which was in favour of the rich and against the poor man; he called him a Nero and a Caligula for such a measure, etc.

He then advised the people to organize to resist the draft and appoint their leader, and if necessary he would be their leader (uproarious cheers). Immediately after, the mob destroyed a beautiful dwelling at Lexington Avenue and 47th Street. And they did organize. Mounted leaders were seen to give orders to subordinate leaders of mobs; one of these mounted men rode on horseback into the hardware store of Hiram Jelliffe in Ninth Avenue and seized what arms and powder he had. Mr. Jelliffe afterwards identified him as a clerk in one of the City departments.

Governor Horatio Seymour, in answer to a call from Washington, had hurried off the militia to Pennsylvania. He made a memorable speech standing upon the City Hall steps, in which he addressed the rioters as "my friends." A report of it says:

> Standing near him on the steps was a ring-leader of a mob, who had just made an inflammatory speech and who had recently come from an assault on the *Tribune*.

The *Tribune* (editorially) said practically that:

the sending of the militia out of New York was with a knowledge that it would be desirable to have them away when his (the Governor's) 'friends' wanted to riot.

I am aware that Governor Seymour has been a sort of idol with many, and that if I lay my poor weak tongue on his fair name, I will incur their displeasure; but I have always disliked shams.

Not wishing to be tedious, I want to recall that when the war broke out the Confederacy was thoroughly equipped to take its place as a fully organized nation at once. This fact was commented on and efforts were made to explain how it was accomplished. No comprehensive history of the struggle can be written that does not include the secret societies that abetted. They played as important a part as did the army which opposed us, and was vastly more dangerous by reason of the insidious character of its movements.

One State after another swung into line under some mysterious talisman, although there was a strong sentiment against leaving the Union.

In delving into affairs generally, I became possessed of information that, so far as I know, has never been in print. I learned that a secret organization known as the "Knights of the Golden Circle" was the nucleus of the Confederacy. That under its secret fostering the Confederacy was fully developed, ready to take its place among the nations. That the Knights were an outgrowth of the defunct "Know Nothing" society that had become disrupted on the subject of the extension of slavery (which also divided churches). That as soon as the Confederacy was in the saddle, no longer were there any initiations into the "Knights of the Golden Circle," but a subordinate society was organized to do further work, i. e., to further disrupt the Union. This society was known as the "Sons of Liberty."

The purpose of the "Sons of Liberty" was to form a northwestern confederacy. My source of information said that it was understood in that circle, that Governor Horatio Seymour was to give the signal for disruption, which was to be a refusal from New York to furnish its quota of soldiers. Seymour failed them. He did not refuse, but he protested and procrastinated. He obstructed the draft as adroitly as he could, claiming inequities. And on August 7th, 1863, Mr. Lincoln in a communication to Seymour regarding these claims, said: "We are contending with an enemy who, as I understand, drives every ablebodied man he can reach into his ranks, very much as a butcher drives bullocks into a slaughter pen; no time is wasted, no argument is used."

And Mr. Lincoln repeatedly wrote Governor Seymour of the cost in blood and treasure by the delays he was causing.

The bloodiest and most brutal riots this country ever saw ensued in New York, Boston, Portsmouth and other cities. The draft riots were, in fact, but the first step of the "Sons of Liberty" in uprising, towards forming another rupture. To this secret movement of the "Sons of Liberty" I refer to the following documents:

Head Quarters, District of Indiana,
Indianapolis, Sept. 3, 1864.

1st. Large numbers of men of suspected loyalty to the United States, have heretofore, and still are immigrating to the State of Indiana, and in some localities their open and avowed hatred to the Government, and treasonable designs are fully expressed. .

By order of
Bvt. Major General Alvin P. Hovey,
And. C. Cemper, A.A.G.

An order had previously been issued by General Heintzelman, Commander of the Department, prohibiting the transport of arms into the Department by Railroads.

Governor Oliver P. Morton, in his message to the Legislature in June, 1865, said:

Some misguided persons who mistook the bitterness of party patriotism and ceased to feel the obligations of allegiance to our Country and Government, conspired against the State and National Government and sought by Military force to plunge us into the horrors of revolution.

A secret organization had been formed which by its lectures and rituals inculcated doctrines subversive of the Government, and which carried to their consequences would evidently result in disruption and destruction of the nation.

The members of this organization were united by solemn oaths, which if observed, bound them to execute the orders of their Grand Commanders without delay or question, however treasonable or criminal might be their character.

I am glad to believe that the great majority of its members regarded it merely as a political machine and did not suspect the ulterior treasonable action contemplated by its leaders, and upon discovery of its true character, hastened to abjure all connection with it.

Some of the chief conspirators have been arrested and tried by the government, and others have fled, their schemes have been exposed and baffled.

The arrest of Clement L. Vallandigham, of Ohio, for treason, uncovered part of the conspiracy; he was, in fact, the Grand Commander of the Order. Of him Mr. Lincoln said:

I solemnly declare my belief that this hindrance of the military, including maiming and murder, is due to the course in which Mr. Vallandigham has been engaged, in a greater degree than to any other cause, and it is due to him personally, in a greater degree than to any other man.

The Indianapolis *Journal*, July 2nd, 1864, said:

Members of the Sons of Liberty were advised that Morgan (the Rebel raider) would be in Kentucky, and Vallandigham in Hamilton, on or about June 14th (1864). It was through information furnished by members of this order that Governor Bramlette of Kentucky was apprised of Morgan's intended raid and attack upon Frankfort.

The rumour that there was collusion between the friends of Vallandigham and Morgan seems possible. In the letter of Governor Bramlette, which we append, significant allusion is made to it. It would seem strange indeed, that the Sons of Liberty should be so advised of the simultaneous raids of the Canadian and Kentucky Confederates unless a common understanding was had between the two traitors, and concerted action determined upon. That they were so advised is evident from the fact that certain of their number admonished Governor Morton of Indiana beforehand, who in turn advised Governor Bramlette of the approaching danger in time for him to provide for it.

Commonwealth of Kentucky,
Executive Department,
Frankfort, June 22, 1864.

Governor Oliver P. Morton,
    Indianapolis, Ind.

Dear Sir.—I return you my most grateful thanks for your prompt assistance during Morgan's recent raid. The timely arrival of the 43rd Regiment, Indiana Volunteers, gave us entire relief against apprehension of danger.

Although the citizens had repulsed the Rebels, yet the large numbers still infesting this section at the time of their arrival kept us upon constant vigil and serious apprehension of another assault.

The patriotism and kindly feeling which prompted the gallant veterans of the Forty-third to rush to our relief without delaying after their long and arduous labours to even greet their families, deserves the highest commendation from their countrymen, and will ever command from us of Kentucky, the profoundest gratitude.

The appearance of Vallandigham, of Ohio, simultaneously with Morgan's raid in Kentucky, fully confirms the matter made known to me through General Lindsey, by you.

The defeat of Morgan has frustrated their movements for the present, but vigilance in the future must still guard us against the machinations of evil doers.

Yours truly,
Thomas E. Bramlette.

Arms for the Sons of Liberty were seized in Indianapolis and New York, and at many other places. The organization was said to have a membership of one million members, all bound, by oath, to sustain the Southern Confederacy.

In many instances, to outward appearances, they were merely social or political clubs that could be attended by the unsuspecting, when they were not in executive session.

The draft riots, hotel burnings, attempts to destroy our water supply, and kindred work, down to and including the assassination conspiracy, are all to be charged to the Sons of Liberty. They are also to be charged with the presidential election fraud of 1864. Its virus permeated all. No man has ever admitted being a member of it.

And Governor Seymour was expected to be its "bell wether" in the disruption movement. Evidently his nerve failed him. The riots in New York probably demonstrated to him that real war is real h———l, and it scared him. I do not assume that any considerable portion of the Confederates were members of either of the secret societies; soldiers are seldom conspirators.

There were characters in the Confederate service whom a Union man could well admire: Lee, "Stonewall" Jackson, Alexander H. Stevens and others, but there should be contempt only for men who, while holding office under the protecting arm of a magnanimous government, bent every nerve to trip up their benefactor.

Uncle Burdette's service was exclusively with troops. First with the 90th Regiment at Key West (Graham has yet a bottled scorpion that he sent home from there, found in his sleeping blanket), then with the 16th Cavalry in Virginia, and finally with the 162nd Regiment in the assault on Port Hudson. He was also with the Banks Red River expedition. No better man ever straddled a horse; he could have acquitted himself as a champion "bronco buster."

The following incident belongs right here:

Headquarters, Fort McHenry, Md.,
Sept. 18th, 1863.

Special Order No. 190.

Lieut. H. B. Smith, of Co. D, 5th N.Y. Arty, with a guard from Co. G., N.Y. Arty., consisting of one sergeant, two corporals and twenty-two men, with two days rations, will, when transportation is provided, proceed to Alexandria, Va, in charge of ninety-three soldier prisoners, and turn them over with lists and charges of same to the commanding officer of Camp of Distribution, near that place.

2. This duty performed Lieut. Smith and guard will return without delay and report to the commanding officer of this post. Lieut. Thos. Grey, the quarter master, will furnish the necessary transportation.

By command,
Col. P. A. Porter.
Ford Morris,
1st. Lieut. 6th N.Y. Arty.
Post Adjutant.

Lieut. Smith,
D. Co., 5th N.Y. Arty.

On our way to Washington, at Laurel, Md., we found the railroad bridge crossing the Patuxent river had been washed away by a recent freshet. We were forced to disembark, go down a high embankment and cross the river by a foot bridge. By some means some of the prisoners had obtained some "fire water" and were troublesome; some of them were fighting on this foot bridge. I took a hand in it and tumbled a few into the river (not very deep). Just then I noticed three or four of them scurrying away, running through a field of grain. I really felt more sorry for the owner of the field than for the loss of the men.

"THE MAPLES", LAUREL, MD.

Aunt Mag had often spoke of our visiting her brother William and sister Mary at Laurel, but we never went there until after our marriage, when I found, on arriving there, that the owner of the grain field my prisoners had so ruthlessly damaged was brother William. He could not remember the instance, as such events were of frequent occurrence, but we had a laugh over it.

Somewhat a History
of My Early Life

I was on duty with troops until detailed as Assistant Provost Marshal at Fort McHenry. The administration of prisoners confined at Fort McHenry had become unsatisfactory; escapes were frequent. Colonel Porter selected Capt. Holmes of the 8th New York Heavy Artillery and myself to reform the prison.

Headquarters, Fort McHenry,
October 25, 1863.
General Order No. 51.
1. Lieut. George Nellis, Co. D., 5th Arty., N.Y.V., is hereby relieved from duty as Asst. Provost Marshal and will without delay report to his Company Commander for duty.
2. Lieut. H. B. Smith, Co. D., 5th Arty., N.Y.V., is hereby appointed Asst. Provost Marshal and will without delay assume the duties of that office.

P.A. Porter,
Col. 8th N.Y.V. Arty.
Com. Post.

Lieut. H. B. Smith,
D. Co., 5th Reg., N.Y.V., Arty.,
Fort McHenry, Md.

Right here was begun what led up to my ultimately becoming a full-fledged secret service operator. Born in the green foot-hills of the Catskill Mountains (near where Rip Van Winkle dozed), I learned my "A B abs" in the little brown school house at Cornwallville. Father died when I was four years old. Mother traded the farm for some

New York tenements, and we all located there, when I was ten years old. I attended the public schools where I was properly "hazed" and got what was "coming" to all country boys; finally I graduated under the tutelage of Dr. Joseph Finch (a patriot indeed, who made a lasting impress for earnestness on thousands of boys), and then went to business as an entry clerk with a large importing metal house, where I remained until the war broke out.

You will therefore see I had had no former experience (my age was 22 years) and whatever wit I had for such service was inborn or home-made. Zeal I know I had; perhaps its birth was from a chalk legend some pedagogue had inscribed over the door-frame in the little brown school house, reading: "What man has done, man can do." At any rate I have remembered it.

My education in the burning political questions had been sharply marked by the presidential campaign of 1860. My brothers, A. P. and Burdette, were "Douglas" Democrats. My fellow clerk, Clarence W. Meade (later Judge Meade), was a "Bell and Everett" Democrat. I was a born "Lincoln" Republican. So between the discussions at the house and the office, I was somewhat sharpened.

I remember how I struggled against their arguments that Lincoln was an uneducated, uncultured rail-splitter. I knew of his discussions with Douglas, but never did I completely vanquish them until Mr. Lincoln delivered his Gettysburg oration, and "that ball fetched all the pins and knocked a hole through the alley." And it must be noted that I thought myself, somewhat like a Demosthenes, for I had practiced in that little school house on "Twinkle, Twinkle, Little Star" and two verses of "On Linden When the Sun Was Low," much to mother's delight. So equipped, or so not equipped, I began my duties as Assistant Provost Marshal.

Confederate mail carrying, spy promoting, blockade promoting, recruiting for Confederate service, were being engineered right from among these prisoners. I "under-grounded" it all. Through this channel I enlisted for the Confederate service. Of course you know that when I enlisted in the service of our enemies, I did so to discover their actions, and was what most people call a "spy." I had often read the story of Nathan Hale, the splendid patriot of the American Revolution who was a spy in the service of General Washington and who gave up his life to the service. (The Sons of the Revolution of the State of New York have erected a fine monument to him in the New York City Hall Park).

Perhaps there would be less danger in being a soldier in the ranks who goes forward with arms in hand and fights openly in battle and dies thus, than to be a spy and constantly in the shadow of death, night and day, and no soldier's death for him, but the death of the hangman's noose; yes, I knew all this.

I worked a blockade running outfit, involving General Morris's adjutant general, Capt. E. W. Andrews (of whom I will tell more later on), and I captured Confederate mail carriers, none of which were any part of my duty, but all contributed to the general good of the service. Strictly speaking, my duties were completed by caring for the safe keeping, discipline and comfort of the prisoners in our charge. To do more was supererogation, and ought to be credited to zeal.

In a short time I found that these Confederates worked their escape through the use of gold supplied them by their sympathizers in bribing the guards. But we stopped that and thereafter the soldiers for sentry duty at certain posts were selected for their known probity. Escapes continued for a time (but they were always recaptured when they supposed themselves safe outside our guards).

When these escapes (?) were accomplished there was great jubilation among the Confederates. They had a great "laugh" on the Yankees; which laugh was changed to "the other side of the mouth" when all the escaped (?) ones were marched back into camp, one bright morning. About a mile down the road leading from our exterior gate to Baltimore was a hotel called the "Vineyard." I engaged the upper floors of it in which to domicile my escaped (?) prisoners. When we had accumulated there about fifteen we marched them all back to our prison.

After telling their fellows of the futility of their plans no more escapes were attempted.

The government was kind to prisoners. We clothed them and gave them blankets to keep them comfortable. I have receipted rolls now showing such issues. They came to us in rags or worse than rags, in fact, and left us fat and well clothed. On one occasion when an exchange of prisoners was ordered, I judged that one good suit of clothes was enough to start them off with; but orders came from Washington to allow them to carry away all the clothing given them by their friends, which in some instances was three or four suits to a man.

Our prisoners were confined in buildings known as the Ringgold Battery Barracks, quite insecure for the purpose. We constructed about the premises a plank fence twelve feet high, with balcony and sentry boxes on top, leaving no good chance for communication between prisoners and guards.

The first unpleasant duty devolving on me is described in the following order:

Headquarters, Fort McHenry,
Nov. 19. 1863.

General Order No. 53.

In pursuance of General Order No. 54 and 56 issued from Headquarters, Middle Department, 8th Army Corps, Oct. 26, and Nov. 3, 1863, and General Order No. 92, issued from headquarters 2nd. Separate Brigade, Defences of Baltimore, Nov. 19, 1863, William F. Gordon, a prisoner in confinement at this post, will be shot to death with musketry, between the hours of 12 m. and 3 o'clock p. m., on Friday, the 20th inst., on the Parade Ground at Fort McHenry, according to military usage in such cases, provided the approval of the President of the United States be received.

The Asst. Provost Marshal of the Post, Lieut. H. B. Smith, is charged with the execution of this order.

(Signed)   By Command of
Col. P. A. Porter,
8th N.Y.V. Arty., Com'd'g Post.

Geo. Wiard,
Lieut. 8th N.Y.V. Arty and Post Adjt.

A harder duty could not be directed. In cases where execution is by shooting, a firing party is picked, and their rifles are loaded for them. One gun among them is loaded with a blank cartridge, so that each member of the firing party can hope he has it.

In case death does not result from the firing it becomes the duty of the officer commanding the firing party to complete the execution of the order. That was not a cheerful prospect for me. I had twenty-four hours for serious contemplation; suppose the men should aim wrong? Then I would be compelled to shoot the man as a mere cold duty. We were spared its execution by the following telegraphic order:

War Department,
Nov. 20, 1863.

Major General Schenck:

The President directs that the execution of sentence of death against Gordon, now in Fort McHenry, be suspended until further orders.

(Signed)   E. M. Stanton,
Sec. of War.

A Flattering Endorsement
by Colonel Porter

For the purpose of showing how I grew in the service I will ask you to read each order carefully. Sometimes they explain themselves, sometimes not.

Investigations started in the prisons required work to be done outside the garrison, throughout Maryland and perhaps into Virginia, which would carry me outside our post limits and required authority from Department commanders. The Department comprised Maryland, parts of Delaware and Virginia. The following personal letter was addressed to Colonel W. S. Fish, Provost Marshal under General Schenck:

Headquarters, Fort McHenry,
Nov. 27, 1863.

Dear Colonel.—Our Assistant Provost Marshal, Lieut. Smith, has got hold of a sloop and her Captain. He was to be examined before you, but Smith says that McPhail's men have other and earlier accounts to settle with him. I suggest this as you may have a great deal to do and may prefer to transfer the case to those already familiar with it.

Very truly,
P. A. Porter,
Col. 8th N.Y.V. Arty.,
Com'd'g Post.

The following will show my progress in such matters:

Headquarters, Middle Department,
8th Army Corps.
Office Provost Marshal,
Baltimore, Dec. 23, 1863.

Lieut. H. B. Smith, Assistant Provost Marshal, Fort McHenry, is hereby authorized to visit and search any house in the City of Baltimore that he has good reason to believe contains Rebel mail, or any treasonable matter.

By order,
W. S. Fish,
Col. and Provost Marshal General,
8th Army Corps.

My work at Fort McHenry absolutely required freedom to act outside.

Office Provost Marshal,
Fort McHenry, Jan. 8, 1864.

Confidential.
Colonel Fish,
Provost Marshal, 8th Army Corps.

Dear Sir.—I am at last able to report that we have gotten underway an underground correspondence between Trought and Emmerich. At first the correspondence was unimportant (which was, of course, policy for them), but now they have become confidential. I, with some others, intend to enlist in the Rebel service, but my plan is too long to explain here.

Now, Colonel, if you will drop a line to Colonel Porter, asking him to allow me to organize a squad of reliable men, say twelve or fifteen, and instruct them, whom we can call upon at any time, we will guarantee to show some rich developments inside of three weeks.

Emmerich is not alone but is connected with some of the largest houses in Baltimore.

Trusting this will meet your approval, I am, Col.

Very resp'y,
H. B. Smith,
Lt. and Asst. Pro. Mar.

This was officially approved first by Colonel Fish, and then by Colonel Porter.

Office Provost Marshal,
Fort McHenry, Jan. 26, 1864.

Col. P. A. Porter,
Commanding 2nd Separate Brigade,
Defences of Baltimore.

I respectfully beg leave to lay before you the following and ask for authority to proceed further.

Four recruits for the Rebel Army are in Baltimore, also two Rebel officers. I want authority to follow them and make the arrest when about to cross the Potomac, thus implicating all the parties connected in recruiting for the Rebel Army in and about Baltimore. I have it so arranged that it will be impossible for them to get away from me, if I am allowed to proceed. And as I have some more operations in process of development, I would respectfully ask to have the authority extended to cover them also.

I could make some of these arrests in Baltimore, but as it is perfectly safe, by allowing them to get a little further, it would make the case a still more fatal one for the parties concerned.

I am, Colonel, Very Resp'y,
Your Ob'd't Serv't,
H. B. Smith,
Lt. and Asst. Pro. Mar.

The endorsement on the back of the above paper has always been a source of gratification. No man from New York State was ever more highly esteemed than Colonel Porter. He was talked of for Governor. A brave, true, and generous man, loved by all. He was killed at Cold Harbor, leading his regiment. His body was dragged back to our lines in the darkness of the night.

Headquarters, 2nd Separate Brigade,
Defences of Baltimore.
Jan. 26, 1864.

I approve of the proceedings of Lieut. Smith, who has my entire confidence as an upright and skilful officer. I have referred him to the Provost Marshal for advice, instruction, and authority.

P. A. Porter,
Col. 8th N. Y. V. Arty.,
Commanding 2nd Separate Brigade.

On the same day the application was approved at Department

Headquarters.

The centre around which this recruiting and other disloyal schemes revolved was one Christian Emmerich, a fashionable shoemaker on South Gay Street. His place was a convenient centre for all important Confederate sympathizers. His residence was in a fashionable part of the city. We were entirely successful, capturing the whole party, including a conductor on the Baltimore and Ohio Railroad, who was caught transporting these recruits, well knowing their character. We simultaneously seized the Christian Emmerich store on South Gay Street, and his residence; in the latter we found much incriminating evidence, such as orders for Confederate uniforms, gold braid, buttons and Confederate letters. Emmerich was not a common mender of "old soles," but was the shoemaker to the bon-ton of Baltimore. We entirely destroyed the Confederate recruiting business conducted through that channel.

I have a photograph of the conductor referred to, taken together with his pal or partner, who was a spy. The spy's name was Charles E. Langley. I will tell you all about him and his mysterious backing when I come to my regular work in December, 1864, where his statement is printed.

Investigator's Education

In our prison were confined prisoners of all classes, Confederate officers, spies, blockade-runners, pirates, civil and political prisoners. Our office was the reception room where these persons interviewed their "sympathizers," much of such interviewing taking place in my presence. Their mail passed through our hands, what better place could there have been to develop an "investigator?"

War Department,
Washington, Feb. 27, 1864.

General Morris, commanding at Fort McHenry, will allow Mr. W. G. Woodside to see Thomas I. Hall and —— Baylor, Rebel prisoners confined there. General Morris will be present at the interview.

By order of the Secretary of War.

(Signed)   C. A. Dana,
Asst. Secy. of War.

This was endorsed:

To the Provost Marshal:
You will allow Mr. W. G. Woodside, the bearer of this, to see the prisoners mentioned within, Hall and Baylor. Lieut. Smith will be present at the interview.

(Signed)   P. A. Porter,
Col. 8th N.Y.V. Arty.,
Commanding-Brigade.

Fort McHenry, Feb'y 28, 1864.

Baltimore, Feb'y 15, 1864.

Sir.—Will you be kind enough to deliver the joined letter to Jules Klotz, a French subject, detained at Fort McHenry. He wrote to me to direct my letters to yourself.

I should be very obliged to you to let me know the reasons why he has been arrested and his true situation towards the American government.

Very respectfully yours,

(Signed)   A. Sauvan,

French Vice Consul.

To Mr. Smith,
Lieutenant, Fort McHenry.

You will see by these documents that my survey of prisoners and their letters was always by authority and not merely to gratify my own curiosity.

The Adjutant General is the confidential reliance of a commanding officer. General Morris was advanced in years and depended implicitly on his Adjutant General, Captain E. W. Andrews. I branded Andrews *a traitor to the colors*. It was a serious position for a subaltern to assume, but I had the evidence to substantiate the charge. In searching the house of one Terrence R. Quinn, a noted blockade-runner, then a prisoner in Fort McHenry, I found evidence that Andrews was a partner in his crimes. And I found that my predecessor, the former Assistant Provost Marshal, was also incriminated; then it became easier for me to understand how so many prisoners had been allowed to escape (as many as sixty-five in one night). Later on I will have two more references to Andrews, which will explain what became of him.

Andrews was a man of brains. He started in life, I believe, as a minister of the gospel, then turned to law. By his suavity and impudence, he gained control of General Morris. The post was important because it carried so great a number of prisoners. Andrews had his son made Provost Marshal, and the escapes of prisoners by one means or another, were made so easily that the scandal of it had appeared in many Southern newspapers. When I finally imprisoned Andrews on General Sheridan's order, in his half intoxicated condition he admitted his Confederate sympathies.

A Storm on the Chesapeake

My initial trip down the Chesapeake Bay after blockade-runners was made under the following order:

> Headquarters, Middle Department,
> 8th Army Corps,
> Baltimore, Mch. 22, 1864.

Special Order No. 73.

2nd Lieut. H. B. Smith, 5th Regt. N. Y. Artillery, is hereby ordered to proceed down the Eastern shore, Virginia, and arrest —— Jacobs (citizen) and such other persons as may be found in company with him. If Lieut. Smith has reason to believe that they are engaged in the practice of smuggling or running the blockade, and seize all contraband goods in their possession.

Lieut. Smith will seize and hold the following named vessels, *viz*.: Schooners *Trifle, Frances E. Burgess, Despatch, Washington,* and *Glib,* wherever he may find them, and will convey them to the nearest place of safety within our lines.

Lieut. Smith will assume command of the steam tug placed at his disposal by orders from this office, and having accomplished the object of this order will return to this city, and make immediate report to the Commanding General.

Lieut. Smith is permitted to use his discretion as to the disposition of the vessels named in case of emergency. By command of

> Major General Lew Wallace,
> (Signed)   Sam'l B. Lawrence,
> Asst. Adj. Gen'l.

Quinn, the prisoner referred to above was out on parole and was thus able to pursue his business. He was in the habit of purchasing much of his supplies from a certain ship chandler on Pratt street, a friend of mine, and, in fact, a good Union man, who so concealed me in his premises that I learned much of Quinn's plans from his (Quinn's) own mouth; and this order was to enable me to develop the matters he had disclosed.

Blockade running, mail carrying and "spy" carrying, along the Potomac and Chesapeake, was carried on in such a cute manner as to necessitate a peculiar service to meet and stop it. Gunboats nor troops could baffle it; it was done in skiffs, canoes (called *cunnas*), small sail boats with dirty sails hardly to be seen in broad daylight. These little "creepers" would run right up under the bows of gunboats unnoticed; as soon as shore was touched, if a plug was pulled out of the bottom of a boat it would immediately and entirely submerge itself, until wanted for use again.

The price for carrying one person across the river was fifty dollars in gold, which tempted to the business the most dare devil men on either side of the line. As to merchandise, the plan was to "work" the local storekeepers, for in the North it was perfectly legitimate to allow all the merchandise desired to go to the line just on the borders of territory patrolled by us, which might be only an hour's sail with fair wind to put it at night within the reach of the Confederates. These stores were not in villages, as was the case further north, but were isolated, very frequently on a cross road in the woods.

Oystering was a favourite cloak for blockade-runners. Sometimes vessels of little value (three hundred dollars or so) were loaded in Baltimore with goods and purposely *swamped* on the south side of the river to allow the Confederates to confiscate. I was "on the inside" once when a captain was offered fifteen thousand dollars to allow his vessel to be loaded and to permit its destruction when in reach of the Confederates.

There was some delay in the preparation of my written report which caused anxiety at headquarters, which was expressed in the following:

Headquarters, Middle Department,
8th Army Corps, Baltimore,
Apl. 5, 1864.

Colonel.—I am directed by Major General Wallace to request you to inform him what is the latest information you have concerning Lieut. H. B. Smith, 5th N.Y. Arty., who was sent with a squad of men on the 22nd ult. to make certain seizures. Please state near what point he was last known to be.

Resp'y your ob'd't serv't,

Sam'l B. Lawrence,

A. A. G.

To Col. Porter,

Com'd'g 2nd Sep. Brigade.

The above I find among my papers. I cannot understand it in view of the fact that I reported March 30th (see following), and was appointed Chief of the Secret Service by General Wallace on April 3rd. The years are many since then and it is hard to remember details, but my present theory is that as General Wallace had but recently assumed command, the Adjutant General's office was in confusion. "I am directed by Major General Wallace" is the usual language for an *Adjutant General* to use; at any rate my report is dated March 30th, and I was interviewed by General Wallace on April 2nd, this I clearly remember.

Fort McHenry, Mch. 30, 1864.

To the General Commanding,

8th Army Corps, Middle Department.

General.—I have the honour to report that in compliance with Special Order No. 73, Mch. 22, 1864, I proceeded with a guard of 12 men on board the steam tug *Adriatic*, but on account of the weather did not leave until the morning of the 23rd.

I was alongside the Cutter (*Revenue*) and notified the officer commanding to arrest any of the vessels named in my order. I was afterwards hailed, and ran back to the Cutter again, and learned that the schooner *Frances E. Burgess*, Capt. J. J. Lewis, had left just one-half hour before. On the morning of the 22nd, she came in and just touched at the wharf, immediately dropping out in the stream. This last fact, connected with the previous one, also the fact that Quinn was much worried about the "F. E. B." led me to believe that the *Burgess* was not all right, and that Captain Lewis had learned of my moves and had attempted to evade me. I made chase for her.

At Hill's Point (below the Choptank River) I arrested the schooner *Trifle*, and took her in tow to Point Lookout. By her papers she is with bonds given by E. R. Quinn, T. R. Quinn, and George G. Nellis, stated in her license, dated Feb'y 3, 1864.

Her enrollment dated Feb'y 3rd, 1864, shows that T. R. Quinn, master, is a citizen of the United States, and had sworn to it, when he was then on his parole as being a British subject.

Her crew consisted of Captain Seward, Farrell, Reddick, Zervicks, and Bailey, deck hands. Captain Seward has acknowledged that he ran the blockade, and that he was in Richmond about last Christmas, but did not go on this vessel. I believe the balance of the crew are innocent men. I found Bailey to be of great service to me on the balance of my trip.

I remained at Point Lookout on the night of the 23rd. On the 24th, went up to St. Mary's River for a harbour, on account of a heavy blow. On the evening of the 24th, I started for and arrived at Pocomoke Sound (Accomac), where we remained that night. On the 25th, went into Onancock Creek, where I landed with eight men, and sent the Steamer around to the Pungateague River to wait for us. In the evening we arrived at the house of one T. W. Jacobs, on the sea side. We entered and searched his house; next morning we learned our error, and although he is undoubtedly a Rebel, I released him.

We then made our way to the house of one William E. Jacobs, on the bay side, where we arrived at 3 p. m., on the 26th. At this place I found the schooner *Frances E. Burgess*—Captain Lewis. I arrested Mr. Jacobs, and found him to be the man engaged with Quinn. I searched his house and barns but found nothing contraband, as they had been duly warned by the arrival of the *Burgess*.

Captain Lewis stated that he left Baltimore on the 11th of March, and arrived at Accomac Creek on the 14th, and said that was his last trip. Mr. Jacobs made same statement.

Captain Lewis was arrested about last June, about the same time that Quinn was arrested. He said that he was caught in the act of leaving the Eastern shore with contraband goods and that his intention was to run the blockade; he said he was examined by Captain E. W. Andrews, and afterwards released after taking the oath of allegiance.

Both Jacobs and Lewis say that Lieutenant Andrews, Captain Andrews' son, was to go into business on the Eastern shore; that they engaged two stores for the purpose, but that Andrews did not come down there.

Mr. Jacobs said that Quinn had often remarked that he could

get anything done at Fort McHenry with the Adjutant General. At first both Jacobs and Lewis denied all knowledge of any man named Andrews.

Jacobs said that J. J. Hodge (the writer of some of the letters found in Quinn's possession) was arrested on the Eastern shore about the same time that he and Quinn were, on the charge of attempting to go south; said that he heard Quinn speak of letters that he had from Hodge, but did not know their contents. Quinn was the first man that employed him (Lewis) after his release, and said it was Quinn's own seeking (to employ a man of that character appears rather suspicious).

The creek where we found the *Burgess* is one that no steamer can enter, or even a sailing vessel, unless piloted by an old residenter of that neighbourhood. The creek is very crooked and the channel is very narrow.

All the people about that country seem to be very closely united and watch a stranger's movements very closely. On the evening of the 27th, we left this creek with the schooner, and on the afternoon of the 28th, we arrived in the Pungateague, and started on the steamer, towing the schooner for Point Lookout, where we arrived at 9 p. m.

On the morning of the 29th we left the Point with the two schooners, but afterwards let go the *Burgess*, and sent her up under sail to Baltimore, where she arrived at 4 p. m., after encountering a very heavy sea. We arrived here at 9.20 p. m.

I could find nothing of the schooners *Despatch* or *Glib*, I made many inquiries for the schooner *Washington*, but could not find her.

On our way back to the city Captain Seward, of the *Trifle* said that there was a sign "Washington" painted on it, in the hold of the *Trifle*, which I afterwards found to be true. I think by the actions of all connected, that "Washington" was sometimes substituted for *Trifle*; this sign was hid away and only by accident found.

Both the *Burgess* and *Trifle* have been confiscated before, two or three times.

I have this day been on the Cutter, twice, to ascertain to a certainty if the *Burgess* left on the 23rd inst., and the officers say they will swear she passed out on that day; that she was in here I know. I then went to the Custom House and found that she did not enter or clear on that trip but left without any papers, and did not stay in Port over 24 hours.

I have the honour to be,

Very respy. your obdt. servt,

(Signed) H. B. Smith,

Lieut. 5th N.Y. II. A.

Lieutenant Andrews and George G. Nellis, "tied up" to Quinn and Lewis, the blockade-runners, had been, respectively, Provost and Assistant Provost Marshals at Fort McHenry, prior to the assignment of Captain Holmes and myself to those offices.

It pleases me to note how vivid my memory is, after forty-seven years, of the incidents connected with this expedition. Our party of eight, after landing in Accomac, split up, and straggled over the country about ten miles, through fields and timber, in snow and slush nearly ankle deep, avoiding the highways and stopping only at negro huts to inquire our way. We arrived at T. W. Jacobs' house quite late and began our search; right here I want to say our search was orderly, endeavouring not to unnecessarily annoy.

About midnight a great commotion was raised outside the house by the tramping of horses, rattling of sabres, and loud voices. We were surrounded by a troop of cavalry (our cavalry). They were very excited, and they threatened us with everything, until I took the Commandant aside and made him aware of who we were; even then he soundly upbraided me for giving him such a scare. He finally departed.

The next day we went over to the Chesapeake Bay side of the peninsula. When we arrived there we divided into two parties, in order to approach the harbour from two directions. When we arrived on the bluff (about twenty feet above water) my party of four was first to discover that there were a number of sailing vessels at anchor in the little bay. What to do was the question. I determined that we four must capture the whole fleet. Which we did in this way: As quietly as possible we possessed ourselves of one vessel and from it, under the persuasive influence of our revolvers, we compelled the men on all the other vessels to go below deck. Then we searched the vessels in detail, detaining only the *Frances E. Burgess.*

This harbour was an ideal place for such "traders," *i. e.*, blockade-runners. It was perfectly land-locked, could not be seen from the bay, and was very hard to get in or out of; it was impassable for gunboats, and so it was well chosen for the business.

The Chesapeake Bay and its tributaries are indented almost continuously with smaller estuaries, which make excellent hiding places. Beautiful places for residence, and likely spots for romance.

While laying at Point Lookout on our way home a severe March storm came up, dreadful to a land lubber like me. The point is where the Potomac empties into the Chesapeake. Storms are felt there nearly as greatly as at Old Point. It blew so hard I feared it would blow us over onto the wharf. The water was up to the wharf's surface, and there was no sleep for us that night. Next morning, when we started for Baltimore (ninety miles away), as we were rounding the Point a big boiling sea took the yawl of the *Burgess*, davits and all, throwing it high in the air. But to turn back spelled death. Our pilot was Captain Cannon, an old bay pilot. He did not conceal that he was frightened. He said he never had seen such weather. We breasted that storm for about twelve hours. The only encouragement from Captain Cannon was that if our boat could live until we got under the influence of North Point we would be all right; we lived.

The heavens were never more unkind in appearance. I did not spend much time in gazing that way, for the awful waves occupied me. Captain Cannon kept the vessel as near head on as possible, first on top of the wave and then in a trough of the sea. Half the time our screw was revolving in the air. Everything loose on deck washed away. I never had a better chance to contemplate my past and future than in that twelve hours. I remember my great regret was that if we should go down, no one could know what became of us, for I had not reported at Point Lookout and we were unknown on the peninsula. The severity of this storm became a matter of history. Seagoing steamers remained tied to their wharves. The shores of the Chesapeake Bay were strewn with wrecks. The *Adriatic* (our vessel) was iron bottomed and drew six feet of water. The Chesapeake can kick up a sea, give it a northeaster, that would gratify the most hungry tar.

When we were opposite the mouth of the Severn River we saw the steamer *Nellie Pentz* headed out, her bow tossing up and down in the air like a cork. She did not dare come out, to certain wreck, dared not turn around, so she backed up the river again. When we got under the lee of North Point I became courageous and generous; off towards the west was in view a schooner, on the rocks. Her crew of four men were in the rigging. I proposed to Captain Cannon to rescue them. He said it was impossible, as our boat drew more water than theirs and would be wrecked before we could reach them. How-

Major General Lew Wallace

ever, we notified the revenue cutter and they were rescued. When we arrived at Baltimore (nine o'clock p.m.) the wharves were afloat. The big Bay Line steamers, sea-going vessels, had not left the wharf. They had not dared to venture out in the storm our little eighty-foot craft had passed through.

JOHN WOOLLEY

Colonel Woolley

General Wallace assumed command of the Middle Department, 8th Army Corps, March 22nd, 1864. The Department headquarters were located in a large mansion on the northwest corner of Calvert and Fayette Streets, just opposite Battle Monument. I can give no better description of the Department than to quote General Schenck, who formerly commanded there, in his words to General Wallace:

> Your trouble will have origin in Baltimore. Baltimore viewed socially is peculiar. There is more culture to the square block there than in Boston; actual culture. The question of the war divided the old families, but I was never able to discover the dividing line. Did I put a heavy hand on one of the Secessionists, a delegation of influential Unionists at once hurried to the President and begged the culprit off. The most unfortunate thing in connection with the Department and its management is that it is only a pleasant morning's jaunt by rail from Baltimore to Washington. There is another thing you should know, without being left to find it out experimentally, Baltimore is headquarters for a traffic in supplies for the Rebel armies the extent of which is simply incredible. It is an industry the men have nothing to do with. They know better, and leave it entirely to the women, who are cunning beyond belief, and bold on account of their sex. They invent underground lines, too many and too subtly chosen to be picked up by the shrewdest detectives.

General Wallace exactly "fitted the niche," a soldier, lawyer, statesman, and an even tempered man. He so ably administered the Department as to overcome all obstacles. One permanent order was that every prisoner should have a hearing at once. If evidence would stand law, the prisoner was to be held; if not, to be at once released. The Paine case is an apt illustration. I felt sure I could get evidence that he was a spy, but had it not at hand and so had to let him go (I will tell about this later on). There was never a suit for false arrest during General Wallace's administration.

One of my duties was to collate the evidence in cases for trial. I learned what was evidence. I was a witness almost constantly before courts martial and military commissions. It was good experience for me and it has served me ever after in civil life. I am proud to say (but perhaps ought not to) that General Wallace gave me credit for aiding in his able administration of the Department.

No better man could have been found for Provost Marshal General than Colonel Woolley. He was a soldier and a thorough business man.

The Provost Marshal General's Department was located on the southwest corner of Camden and Eutaw Streets. It was in a handsome three-story brick building and had a massive marble entrance. Adjoining it was what had formerly been a slave pen. Between the corner building and the slave pen there was an open court which had been used for the slave mart. The slave pen we used for our prison purposes. The first floor of the main house was used as our public offices. The second floor was General Woolley's headquarters. The third floor was my headquarters. In the rear of the main front corner building was a three-story brick extension, running back about a hundred feet (to an alley) in which were quartered the troops (our guards). The buildings were admirably constructed and centrally located for our purposes.

From now on I was Assistant Provost Marshal General and Chief of the Secret Service. I had a corps of about forty (men and women) under my direction. To illustrate my general lines of work I will give copies of some memoranda which I have. To give all would take more room than I can spare. In looking these memoranda over the greatest gratification I feel comes from the evident fact that I was not a drone, but tried to do my duty. And fifty years further along in our nation's history it may be a satisfaction to my then living relatives to know it.

Confederate General Winder's Detectives

The Secret Service, as its name implies, is the most confidential arm of the service. Its information intelligently guides the commanding general. It gives him to know of the conduct of the enemy and discloses weaknesses, if any exist, in his own armour. There is always a "cloud of mystery" thrown around it by outsiders. But its pursuit, on the inside, is not that of romance, but simply of cold facts; it deals with business propositions. In telling my stories, not being a story writer, I shall tell plain facts, leaving the reader to clothe them with the glamour that a fiction writer would usually apply. Were I to attempt to tell something of all my many stories it would weary a reader; so I will try to select some that are really historic, or interesting from their unusual character.

Provost Marshal's Office,
Fort McHenry, Apl. 10, 1864.

Lieut. H. B. Smith,
Asst. Provost Marshal 8th Army Corps.
I have just been informed by Mrs. Myers that a detective of General Winder's staff from Richmond, Virginia, is in the city in disguise.

Respy.,
J. W. Holmes,
Capt. and Provost Marshal.

General J. H. Winder commanded the Department of Henrico, headquarters at Richmond, Va. Many of his detectives were Marylanders, among them were John Lutz, Wash Goodrich, T. Woodhall,

—— Taylor, and William Byrne.

I perfectly imitated General John H. Winder's signature to passes which we used with success. I had a close imitation of his stationery; only an expert could detect our passes. If he is living I am sure he will pardon the liberty I took, for it was all in the game.

Following is one of General Winder's genuine passes:

Headquarters, Department of Henrico,
Richmond, Va., March 26th, 1864.

Mrs. James Gordon & (3) children, a citizen of Great Britain, having sworn, in good faith, not to reveal, either directly or indirectly, any information that may benefit the enemy, is hereby permitted to pass beyond the limits of the Confederate States, by the route herein designated: and none other. Strictly forbid to pass through General Lee's lines. Go by the lower Rappahannock.

This passport is given, subject in all cases to the approval, delays and restrictions of military commanders through whose lines the persons or person may pass.

By command of the Secretary of War,
Jno. H. Winder,
General Comdg.

Hair: light.
Eyes: blue.
Age: 33.
Complexion: florid.
Height: ——

Our sources of information were numerous, as our own officers were always on duty, and officers in other departments worked in conjunction with us, thus forming an extended net work.

Baltimore, April 14, 1864.

Lt. Smith,

Sir.—I am very unfortunate in always coming when you are out. How has Kremer progressed with the case, anything been done? I go to Washington per order of the Secretary of War. I am obliged to go to New York within two weeks. I wish the case here might be disposed of before I go to New York. Would you oblige me by writing P. O. Box 62, Washington?

Very respy, your obdt servt.,
E. H. Smith, Special Officer, War Dept.

The following is Kremer's report of progress:

United States Military Telegraph,
War Department,
April 17, 1864.

H. B. Smith:

Two men answering description but under different names left here for Leonardtown on the 16th. Shall I follow? If so, answer and send White.

W. V. Kremer.

Headquarters, Middle Department,
April 22, 1864.

Special Order No. 43.

Lieut. H. B. Smith, 5th N.Y. Arty., will proceed to Washington with Mrs. Mary E. Sawyer, Rebel mail carrier, turn her over to Supt. of Old Capitol Prison, taking receipt for prisoner. Will then deliver to Hon. C.A. Dana, Asst. Secy. of War, all the papers in her case, after which he will report without delay at these headquarters.

Quartermasters will furnish transportation.

By command of Major General Lew Wallace.

John Woolley,
Col. and Provost Marshal.

Persons were not disturbed in the enjoyment of their opinions so long as they did not become actively disloyal, but it was my duty to learn who were disloyal for the purpose of keeping them under surveillance. The following report I put in to illustrate that character of work:

Headquarters, Middle Department,
8th Army Corps.
Office Provost Marshal,
Baltimore, Apl. 24, 1864.

H. B. Smith,

Lieut. and Chief:

I have the honour to report that I left Baltimore as per orders and proceeded to Reisterstown and stopped at a tavern and was accosted by a citizen who told me there were detectives in the house, and that he knew I was from the other side, and sent me to a woman named Mrs. Hofman, who keeps a hotel there. I went to her house and represented myself as a Rebel captain.

I had been there a short time when Mrs. Hofman took me upstairs in a bedroom that was in the back part of the house and told me if the detectives came upstairs, to get out of the back window and take a horse that she would have saddled ready for me; she said she did not care for the horse as the citizens would make it up to her.

The detectives did not come upstairs, but a man named C. L. Alder came up to the room and told me to get ready and come down stairs, that he had a buggy ready to see me safe and that he would die before I should be taken and that he had helped many of the Rebels out of just such scrapes by taking them to the Rebel lines.

We went about a mile and a half from Reisterstown and stopped at the house of Dr. J. Larsh, and held a conversation with him and another man that I could not learn the name of; about the best plan for me to adopt was to keep away from the detectives; he, the Doctor, told me that he was very busy or he would take me safe through himself, but told Alder to take me to Charles T. Cockey's, and that he would see me all right.

We then went to C. T. Cockey's and Alder explained to him who I was and Mr. Cockey then introduced me to John C. Brown, of Busson Parish, La., and lately manager of the Rebel Secretary of War's plantation. Mr. Cockey told me to remain there all night and he would see me safe, as he was engaged in the business ever since the war commenced, and had run off a great many men to the Rebel army; in fact he said that men from all parts of the country were sent to him to take across the lines, and that he always went into the Rebel lines with them.

Among the rest that he had taken across was Capt. Simms and Capt. Beard and Gus Williamson. He said when General McClellan was following Lee into Maryland, a man came to him from Washington and gave him the number of men that McClellan had, and the direction he was going to take, and that he went to Frederick, and gave the information to Lee; and would, he said, do so again, if it would do any good to the Southern cause.

Cockey receives papers regularly from Richmond. He also said that Capt. Harry Gilmor stops at his house whenever he comes over the lines, and that a great many men from the South come to his house, and he always helps them. I remained at his house all night, and listened to him and John C. Brown cursing the government for everything they could think of, and telling what they would do if the Rebel army would come into Maryland again. C. T. Cockey was also engaged at the time of Lee's raid into Pennsylvania; he took men to the Rebel army and was in the Rebel lines several times, and gave them all the information that he could get hold of that would do them any good.

Mr. J. C. Brown gave me the name of his brother, Benj. F. Brown, of Frederick, Md., agent for the Baltimore and Ohio Railroad Co., and in charge of the government warehouse which he surrendered to the Rebels without endeavoring to destroy the goods, or to get them out of the way. J. C. Brown told me to go to his brother and let him know who I was and everything would be right, and that he would meet me there with a lot of recruits, and a Rebel mail to take south.

The next day, 21st April, I expressed a wish to go into Pennsylvania for a few days, and promised to meet Mr. Brown in Frederick. Mr. C. T. Cockey took me in his buggy to T. D. Cockey of "I" at Ellingown, near Texas, on the Northern Central Railroad, where I met T. D. Cockey, of "I".

T. Deye Cockey and Philip Fendel, who are violent Rebels, say they have been running men off ever since the war commenced. And T. Deye Cockey says that he has been in the Rebel lines several times, and at one time took three recruits from Harford County to Hanover Junction, when the Rebels were there, and gave them all the information he could.

Richard Worthington, a very wealthy man, whom I met, offered me a horse, and any assistance in his power, to enable me to escape, and stated that he had rented his farm out, and was endeavouring to get his property fixed in such a way that the damned negro government could not confiscate it. He was going to leave the damned Yankees and go to Canada, and from there to Nassau, and take a vessel and go to the Confederacy, where he would be free to do as he pleased. He said he had invested a portion of his money in Confederate bonds, and only wished he had a chance to invest more in them, as the greenbacks, or Yankee shinplasters were not worth a damn.

These men were under the impression that I was the Rebel Capt. Harry Thompson, who, as it was published, had made his escape from a Federal prison. I told them I had escaped from the Old Capitol.

Very respy.,

Wm. V. Kremer,

U. S. D. 8th A. C.

You will notice Mr. Kremer speaks of T. D. Cockey of "I." That is a common way in Maryland and Virginia to designate the lineage of that T. D. Cockey, to obviate confounding him with some other T. D. Cockey.

Later on, in July, when the Confederate Army swung around north and east of Baltimore, the information contained in Mr. Kremer's report became very valuable to us.

Trip on the Steam Tug "*Ella*"

Headquarters, Middle Department,
8th Army Corps,
Baltimore, Apl. 28, 1864.

Special Order No. 48.

Lieut. H. B. Smith, Chief Officer, Secret Service Bureau, 8th Army Corps, will proceed to Washington, D. C., in charge of prisoners, Miss Martha Dungan and Mrs. Key Howard.

On arrival you will deliver prisoners to Mr. Wm. P. Wood, in charge of Old Capitol Prison and receive receipt for same, after which you will report to Hon. C. A. Dana, Asst. Secy. of War, deliver all papers in prisoners' cases and return to these headquarters without delay.

Quartermasters will furnish transportation.

By command of Major General Lew Wallace.

John Woolley,
Lt. Col. and Provost Marshal.

Here is a sad incident illustrating what Hamlet meant when he said: "To what base uses may we return, Horatio!" Mrs. Key Howard, a lineal descendant of Francis Scott Key, author of the "Star Spangled Banner," having obtained a personal pass direct from Mr. Lincoln, permitting her to pass our lines, had actually gathered a Confederate mail, to carry through, under its protection. Honour of a truly "Blue Blood?"—it was absent.

The pass was written on a plain card, and read:

Pass Mrs. Key Howard through the lines.   A. Lincoln.

I might have retained the card, but turned it in with the case. Mrs.

Howard, in discussing with me the lack of honour in so abusing a great favour, became very angry; she said: "Lincoln was vulgar, not a polished man; he sat with legs crossed while talking to me."Young and inexperienced as I was, I was so forcibly struck with the shallowness of *pretended culture* that I have many times told the story to illustrate.

I have no doubt that Mrs. Howard traded upon her family name with President Lincoln. He undoubtedly trusted her, believing that she had honour in her composition. Blockade running schemes were without limit as to variety or manner of evasion.Vessels were loaded in Baltimore, clearing for any port. Trading schooners were loaded, taking shipments for various stores on the rivers and bays of the Chesapeake Bay; some of the shipments would be honest transactions, but others would be especially designed for Confederate consumption.

In April, 1864, the schooner *Wm. H. Travers* (Captain Rice) had been under surveillance. She was loaded at Baltimore with a mixed cargo, part of which was of honest shipments. I learned that it was intended to swamp the vessel within reach of the Confederates, thus permitting them to take the entire cargo regardless of ownership. I allowed its loading and permitted the captain to leave port with her, but after she got well down the stream I overhauled her with the steam tug *Ella*, and brought her back to Baltimore. Her cargo was worth about six thousand dollars. Mr. Blackstone, of St. Mary's County, was the guilty party.

Depot, Quartermaster's Office,
Baltimore, Md., April 30, 1864.

Captain,
    Steam Tug *Ella*:
You will proceed with your tug under the orders of Lt. H. B. Smith, and render such service as he may require; after performing those duties you will return to Boston wharf and report to me.

Respectfully,
A. M. Cummings,
Chief Quartermaster.

Headquarters, Middle Department,
8th Army Corps, Baltimore, May 4, 1864.

H. B. Smith,
    Lt. Comdg. Detective Corps.
Lieutenant.—You will please order the guard in charge of the

schooner *W. H. Travers* to remove and put her in such position at Boston Wharf as will not interfere with the vessels in the government service at the wharf, and not to interfere in any way with or be in the way of the vessels in public service.

I have addressed a note to the Quartermaster asking to be allowed the privilege of unloading the vessel at the wharf.

Very respy,

Your obdt. servt,

John Woolley,

Lt. Col. and Provost Marshal.

Headquarters, Middle Department,

8th Army Corps,

Baltimore, May 11, 1864.

Lieut. Col. Woolley,

Provost Marshal.

Colonel.—I have the honour to report that I have completed the discharge of the goods on board the schooner *W. H. Travers* to the shippers, excepting those named on the enclosed list.

I enclose herewith all the papers in connection with the case, two lists, one of goods not on the manifest, and one of goods not permitted, but on the manifest. I also enclose a note from Mr. McJilton, clerk of the Custom House, showing that some transactions there in this case are not all right.

Mr. McJilton, the Surveyor of the Port, stated that he would not grant a permit for percussion caps, unless by permission of the military authorities. The impression at the Custom House is that the whole transaction of shipping these goods is a fraud, and they do not know what to think of their books and papers.

I have a package of gold leaf in my possession, also two Confederate uniforms. Some of the cotton cards I found stored away in the cabin, and some away under the stairs. The second box on the manifest, shipped by Bolton to R. P. Blackstone, contained one box soap, and one box of glass. I have a certificate from Bolton to that effect. Mr. Passano, who shipped the box containing the glass, denies any knowledge of the contents of the box, as it was a cash bill and he had no record of it.

I am, Colonel,   Very respy your obdt. servt.,

H. B. Smith, Lieut Com'd'g, D. C.

63

We subsequently returned to the innocent shippers their goods, but confiscated the balance, and also the vessel. I afterwards used the *Travers* to capture other blockade runners, and quite successfully. A sailor will recognize a vessel as far as the eye can reach, as surely as a man can recognize any familiar object. She was known as a blockade-runner to the fraternity; we used her to crawl upon others.

Any citizen or soldier from the Confederacy found within our lines was considered a spy; some were executed. To escape such treatment it was necessary to report to the nearest officer and take the oath of allegiance. Even then we were not protected, but had to carefully examine the purported refugee, or deserter, to ascertain their possible honesty. We captured a great many spies.

An official spy, sent out by the Confederates to perform a specific duty, had no conscience to answer to, that would prevent his taking our oath.

Headquarters, Middle Department,
8th Army Corps,
Baltimore May 3, 1864.

Lieut. Col. Woolley,
    Provost Marshal.

Colonel.—I have the honour to report that this evening we arrested James A. Winn, a member of Co. E. 1st Md. Rebel Cavalry, in a house, No. 42 Saratoga street. He was dressed as a citizen; under his coat, with the flaps rolled back, was his uniform jacket. His coat was buttoned, thus hiding his uniform. He wore a black slouch hat.

I placed the inmates of the house, Mrs. Hall and Miss McAlden in arrest, and searched the premises.

Both of these ladies admitted they were aware of Winn's character, and that their sympathies were with the South. I found nothing contraband in the house. They live neatly, but are evidently poor. Miss McAlden remarked that they were too poor to aid the South even if they were so disposed.

I have a guard in charge of the house awaiting your disposition of the case.

Messrs. Allen and Sampson, clerks at Department Headquarters, are, I am informed, boarding at this house.

    I am Colonel,
        Very respy, your obdt. servant,

H. B. Smith,

Lt. Com'd'g D. C.

The papers and pocketbook that I handed you were found on his person.

Any incautious information dropped by Allen or Sampson was likely to be immediately reported to the Confederate authorities. The Department was honeycombed with just such points of insecurity, leaks which it was my duty to stop.

Headquarters, Middle Department,

8th Army Corps,

Baltimore, May 4, 1864.

Col. Woolley,

    Provost Marshal.

Send a good detective to Frederick, Md. He may possibly get track there of some of the 1st (Rebel) Maryland Spies. Send him on the first train.

Lew Wallace,

Major General Commanding.

The above order is in General Wallace's handwriting. Winn, whom we had arrested, was of that regiment and we were searching for others.

John Gillock from Richmond

United States Sanitary Commission,
244 F Street, Washington, D. C.
May 7, 1864.

Lieut. Smith.

Dear Sir.—Your favour was received in due time and after diligent search I am satisfied that no such man is now in Washington; however, I shall keep a close lookout, and any information worthwhile, I shall give you at once.

When you have any business to be done here I shall esteem it a favour to assist you.

Your obdt. servant,
F. M. Ellis,
Chief Detective, U. S. Sanitary Com.

Mr. Ellis's offer of service was without price; in fact there was an entire absence of what is called "commercialism" in those days. Loyalty and zeal were the currency. After three and a half years in such service it was hard for me to get down to a dollars-and-cents business again.

Headquarters, Middle Department,
8th Army Corps,
Baltimore, May 8, 1864.

Lieut. Col. Woolley,
Provost Marshal.

Colonel.—I have the honour to report that Officer Horner arrested William W. Shore, who is, or has been the correspondent of the New York World and News. He says he left Fort Monroe on Feb. 14, and used to forward Rebel papers to New York, until he was ordered away by General Butler.

Enclosed herewith is the telegram on which he was arrested.

I am Colonel,

Very respy. your obdt. servt.,

H. B. Smith,

Lieut. Comdg. D. C.

Headquarters, Middle Department,

8th Army Corps,

Baltimore, May 14, 1864.

Special Order No. 40.

Guard in charge of John Gillock, political prisoner, will proceed to Fort McHenry. On arrival you will report to Commanding Officer, deliver charge with accompanying papers, receive receipt and return to these headquarters without delay.

By command, Major General Wallace.

John Woolley,

Lt. Col. and Provost Marshal.

I remember this young man very well. He was from Richmond. Subsequently, after testing his reliability, I made use of him for detective purposes. He was well acquainted with General Winder's men, hence his value to us.

Governor Seymour's Queer Vigour Appears

> Headquarters, Middle Department,
> 8th Army Corps,
> Baltimore, May 18, 1864.

Provost Guards,
> or U. S. Detectives.

Seize all copies of the New York World of this date, that may arrive from New York, or that you can find in the city.
> By command, Major General Wallace.
> John Woolley,
> Lt. Col. and Provost Marshal.

This order is innocent enough in its appearance, but it is really the executive action upon a subject almost as vital in its effects as any of the great battles of the war.

Under date of May 17th a proclamation, calling for four hundred thousand more troops, purporting to be from President Lincoln, was issued, and was published in certain papers; among them the New York *World*. The following is a copy:

> Executive Mansion, May 17, 1864.

Fellow Citizens of the United States:

In all seasons of exigency it becomes a nation carefully to scrutinize its line of conduct, humbly to approach the throne of Grace, and meekly to implore forgiveness, wisdom, and guidance.

For reasons known only to Him, it has been decreed that this country should be the scene of unparalleled outrage, and this nation the monumental sufferer of the nineteenth century. With a heavy heart, but an undiminished confidence in our cause, I approach the performance of a duty rendered imperative by my sense of weakness before Almighty God and of justice to the people.

It is not necessary that I should tell you that the first Virginia campaign, under Lieut. General Grant, in whom I have every confidence, and whose courage and fidelity the people do well to honour, is virtually closed. He has conducted his great enterprise with discreet ability. He has crippled their strength and defeated their plans.

In view, however, of the situation in Virginia, the disaster at Red River, the delay at Charleston, and the general state of the country, I, Abraham Lincoln, do hereby recommend that Thursday, the 26th day of May, a.d., 1864, be solemnly set apart throughout these United States as a day of fasting, humiliation and prayer.

Deeming, furthermore, that the present condition of public affairs presents an extraordinary occasion, and in view of the pending expiration of the service of (100,000) one hundred thousand of our troops, I, Abraham Lincoln, President of the United States, by virtue of the power vested in me by the Constitution and the laws, have thought fit to call forth, and hereby do call forth the citizens of the United States between the ages of (18) eighteen and (45) forty-five years, to the aggregate number of (400,000) four hundred thousand, in order to suppress the existing rebellious combinations, and to cause the due execution of the laws.

And, furthermore, in case any State or number of States shall fail to furnish by the fifteenth day of June next their assigned quotas, it is hereby ordered that the same be raised by immediate and peremptory draft. The details for this object will be communicated to the State authorities through the War Department.

I appeal to all loyal citizens to favour, facilitate, and aid this effort to maintain the honour, the integrity, and the existence of the National Union, and the perpetuity of popular government.

In witness whereof, I have hereunto set my hand, and caused the seal of the United States to be affixed. Done at the city of

Washington, this 17th day of May, one thousand, eight hundred and sixty-four, and of the independence of the United States the eighty-eighth.

Abraham Lincoln.

By the President:

William H. Seward, Secretary Of State.

This was immediately contradicted by the Government, as follows:

To the Public.

Department of State, Washington, D. C.

May 18, 1864.

A paper purporting to be a proclamation of the President, countersigned by the Secretary of State, and bearing date of the 17th inst. is reported to this Department as having appeared in the New York *World* of this date. This paper is an absolute forgery. No proclamation of this kind has been made, or proposed to be made, by the President, or issued, or proposed to be issued, by the State Department, or any other Department of the Government.

Wm. H. Seward,

Secretary of State.

Under the head "Freedom of Press" *Appleton's Encyclopedia* for 1864 gives twelve columns of space to this matter. The excitement resulted in the greatest distress. Gold advanced four or five *per cent.*, a panic prevailed, and great calamity, of course, followed.

Soon thereafter we seized every telegraph instrument and office record in the Department, and arrested the officers and clerks. I became so tired with the extraordinary labour and loss of sleep, that I actually fell asleep while standing at a desk in one of the offices. I had heard of such experiences, but had believed it impossible.

The object of seizing the newspapers, telegraphic instruments and records, was to prevent the disaster that must follow the further spreading of the impression created by the bogus message, that our Government was in dire distress.

Copperhead conspirators and Confederate agents here and in Canada, had been and were at work to undermine us by every means. Distress to us, however brought about, was their purpose. They sought to create in the minds of the masses the idea that the war was a failure.

These conspirators had tried to use the conscription, in 1863, to disrupt us, and they were again trying to scare the people with a prospective draft, in 1864, to unsettle the public mind before the Presidential election, then soon to occur (in November).

Governor Seymour relentlessly pursued General Dix, seeking to have him indicted for arresting (he claimed) illegally, persons party to the fraud. But the grand jury refused to indict him. Seymour claimed that he (Seymour) was trying to preserve *personal liberty*, from the general government's encroachments, which was also his attitude in Vallandigham's case in 1863.

The New York *World* and *The Journal of Commerce* were the newspapers involved in the affair, but the odium should not attach to the present papers.

The bogus proclamation spread faster and further than the denial of it possibly could.

Arrest of F. W. Farlin and A. H. Covert

Headquarters, Middle Department,
8th Army Corps,
Baltimore, May 21, 1864.

Lt. Col. Woolley,
Provost Marshal.

Colonel.—I have the honour to report the arrest of A. H. Covert and F. W. Farlin, as per order annexed.

I have it from a reliable source that Mr. Alexander Civin went to Philadelphia this morning, I therefore telegraphed to the Provost Marshal there, for his arrest, and to send him under guard to this place.

I am, Colonel,
Very respy. your obdt. servant,
H. B. Smith,
Lieut. Comdg. D. C.

To discover persons engaged in creating sentiments of disloyalty, or in pandering to such sentiments, was a part of our duty; the pulpit was not always loyal.

Headquarters, Middle Department,
8th Army Corps,
Baltimore, May 22, 1864.

Col. Woolley,
Provost Marshal.

Colonel.—I have the honour to report in regard to the sermons of the Reverends Harrison and Poisal: Neither preached a political sermon nor dealt in any way with the affairs of the country, except in one or two instances Mr. Harrison spoke of the present deplorable condition of affairs in this country and seemed to be very much downcast in both preaching and praying. He (Mr. H.) did not utter one word of prayer for our President, Army or Government.

I know of Mr. Poisal's being a correspondent of some of the Rebel prisoners in Fort McHenry.

At both sermons they had very slim audiences.

> I am, Colonel,
>> Very respy. your obdt. servant,
>>> H. B. Smith,
>>>> Lieut. and Chief.

On one occasion it was my duty to attend a State conference in one of the churches; it was rather slimly attended. We were invited to come nearer the altar, and I, with the rest, complied.

We were then asked to in turn arise and announce what district in the State we represented, and report on its condition. I was embarrassed, but kept my eye on the ceiling or on the floor. I presume my dumbness excused me. The closing hymn was No. 701, on page 417, and the first verse was:

Jesus, great Shepherd of the sheep,
To thee for help we fly,
Thy little flock in safety keep,
For O! the wolf is nigh.

They were correct in the guess, about the wolf, but I did not say so out loud.

A very laughable report was made to me by one of my officers who was sent into the country to a meeting in the woods. This officer knew more about guns than about religious meetings. He reported nothing disloyal was said, but urged the necessity of going there next Sunday, as they said: "they would have some big guns there then." The officer was used to guns, and so he assumed that they meant cannons, whereas they were referring to popular speakers who were to be present there the following Sunday.

General Wallace was just the man to administer the affairs of a department so complex in sentiment. No better illustration can be furnished than the following circular letter issued to the churches at a time when the public mind was so wrought up by the assassination of the President. It is too fine a document to be lost. To the General's memory I insert it here:

Headquarters, Middle Department,

8th Army Corps,

Baltimore,Md., April 19, 1865.

Circular.

The conduct of certain clergymen in this city has in some instances, been so positively offensive to loyal people, and, in others, of such doubtful propriety, to say nothing about taste, as to have become a cause of bad feeling with many well-disposed citizens.

As you must be aware, the recent tragedy, so awful in circumstance, and nationally so calamitous, has, as it well might, inflamed the sensibilities of men and women who esteem their loyalty only a little less sacred than their religion.

In this state of affairs you will undoubtedly perceive the wisdom of avoiding, on your own part, everything in the least calculated to offend the sensibilities mentioned. You will also perceive the propriety of requiring members of your congregation, male and female, who may be so unfortunate as to have been sympathizers with the rebellion, not to bring their politics into the church.

So profound is my reverence for your truly sacred profession, that, in the sincere hope of avoiding any necessity for interfering with the exercise of your office, I choose this method of respectfully warning you of the existing state of public feeling, and calling upon you, in the name of our common Saviour, to lend me your influence and energetic assistance, to be exerted in every lawful way, to soothe irritations and calm excitements. You know that what I thus request I have the power to enforce. You ought also to know that, to save the community from the dishonour and consequences of a public outbreak, it would be my duty to exercise all the power I possess, without regard to persons or congregations.

If you feel that you cannot yourself comply with this fraternal solicitation, or that you are unable to control evil-disposed members of your flock, I suggest that it is better, far better, in every respect, that you should close the doors of your church for a season at least.

I have no fear that the kindliness of my purpose in thus communicating with you will be mistaken; and that you may not understand yourself as accused, or specially selected from the mass of your professional brethren, you are informed that a copy of this note has been or will be addressed to every clergyman in the city.

Very respectfully,

Your friend,

Lew Wallace,

Major General Commanding.

The firm referred to in the following two documents was one of the largest stationers in the city. Their reputation for disloyalty was well understood by us. An important part of their business was the dissemination of articles which tended to have the kindergarten effect of schools of disloyalty.

Headquarters, Middle Department,

8th Army Corps,

Baltimore, Md., May 23, 1864.

Lieut. H. B. Smith.

Sir.—We have the honour to report that this afternoon we went into the book store of Kelly & Piet, No. 174 W. Baltimore street, and told them that we were book agents on the Baltimore and Ohio Railroad, and had just arrived from Frederick City. We asked Mr. Piet if he had any books of Abraham Lincoln Trials; he hesitated for a short time, then told us that he had. We then asked him if he had any of the Life of Jackson; he said he had a few, and said he would send and get us some more in half an hour. He then showed us some different books and also some playing cards with the different Rebel Generals on the face of them, which he offered to sell at $4.50 per dozen: also some writing paper and envelopes with the Rebel Flag on, which we bought and you will find the bill enclosed.

We are, Lieut., your obdt. servants,

I. W. Stern and

Geo. R. Redman, U. S. D.

The bill attached was $34.24.

Headquarters, Middle Department,
8th Army Corps,
Baltimore, May 23, 1864.

Col. Woolley,
Provost Marshal.

Colonel.—I have the honour to report that I this day seized and searched the store of Kelly & Piet, No. 174 West Baltimore street, and enclosed hand you a list of contraband articles seized. I also enclose the report of the detectives.

Mr. Piet states that he has been arrested before on a similar charge.

I brought to our office Messrs. Kelly & Piet, but did not lock them up. I have the key of their store in my possession.

I am Colonel,
Very respy. your obdt. servant,
H. B. Smith,
Lieut. Comdg. D. C.

List:

90 Assortments of photos. 212 total.
19 Vols. *Morgan and His Men.*
2 Vols. *Life Stonewall Jackson.*
1 Vol. *1st Year of the War.*
4 Vols. *2nd Year of the War.*
97 Pamphlets *Trial Abraham Lincoln.*
2 Vols. *Rebel Rhymes.*
4 Vols. *Three months in Southern States.*
5 Vols. *Confed. Reports of Battles.*
3 Vols. *Southern History of the War.*
1 Package note paper, Rebel flag.
1 Package envelopes, Rebel flag.
8 Steel Engravings, Rebel Generals.
57 Packages Playing Cards, Confed.

All of this was inflammable matter.

The Captain Bailey, spoken of in the succeeding report, was the same Bailey that I captured in March previous. I had found him to be an excellent sailing master, and a man whom I could trust. The sloop *R. B. Tennis* was one of my fleet.

Office Provost Marshal,
Baltimore, May 28, 1864.

Major H. Z. Hayner,
    Provost Marshal.

Major.—I have the honour to submit the following brief report of the seizure made by sloop *R. B. Tennis*, Capt. Bailey, with three detective officers on board.

Enclosed I hand you report of Detective Lewis, who was placed in charge, which report is not quite so full as it should be, covering all remarks and acknowledgments made by the prisoners.

I will state that they said several times that they were blockade runners by occupation.

Enclosed is the statement made to me by Fred. E. Smith, who, I think, is rather faint hearted in his profession.

Harrison acknowledged to have run the blockade several times, but don't seem willing to talk much, as he thinks "he might implicate some near and dear friends," he has talked a deal to some of the officers, whose statements I shall get when they return to the city.

Alexander refuses to talk, but I shall be able to get it all out of them soon.

I received from Detective Lewis the following which he states was all that was taken from the parties:

Gold and silver, $188.75.

U. S. Currency, $159.00.

Southern States money, $190.00.

Northern States money, $1.00.

1 gold watch. 1 silver watch.

23 large and 2 small boxes tobacco.

1 large yawl boat.

I have stored the tobacco in the store of W. W. Janney, a receipt for which is annexed. The boat is in charge of guard on board the schooner *Travers*.

I will get fuller statements from all the detectives as soon as possible, and give to you. The prisoners are Fred. E. Smith, Powell Harrison and Robert Alexander.

    I am, Major,
        Very respy. your obdt. servant,
            H. B. Smith,
                Lieut. and Chief.

Attached to this report is a memorandum of statements made to me:

Fredk. Smith:

I am from Northumberland County, Va. I left Northumberland County on Wednesday last. I was with Mr. Harrison and Mr. Alexander, no one else with us. I am a citizen. I have been about eight months in Va., all of that time in Northumberland County. I was formerly from Caroline Co., Md.

I started to come North for clothes and things. I had some orders for goods for families in Northumberland County, which I threw overboard after we were hailed, also had twenty odd boxes tobacco.

Mr. Harrison has lived in Northumberland County since I have been there, but has been north of the Potomac three or four times.

I don't know much, of Mr. Alexander, except that he came from Maryland with Mr. Harrison on one of his (Harrison's) trips.

I came over as a passenger with Harrison and Alexander. Some of the tobacco belongs to me. I had about $250 in gold, and about $100 or more in greenbacks, and $50 or $60 in Virginia money. Had no particular point of destination. I was to pay Harrison and Alexander $200 for my fare. I think they intended to land on the Eastern shore, Md., or perhaps on Western shore. I think Harrison and Alexander are blockade runners by profession. They intended to return to Virginia. I think we were about going into Choptank River. I think at about James Point.

I started for Little River, Virginia. I think another party of two or three started at about the same time; they had some tobacco. I did not know their names; they were in a little sloop, dark colour. I saw them again about Point Lookout. I think perhaps they had about two or three thousand pounds. The sloop and sail looked rather old. It was Wednesday night that I last saw the sloop. I think Mr. Harrison was over about three or four weeks since.

Powell Harrison:

Northumberland County, Virginia. I am a farmer, I have lived there about three or four years. I have been north of the Potomac three times since the War.

Robert Alexander:

(Made no statement.)

You will notice the brevity of Harrison's statement, and that Alexander made no statement. Alexander and one other man, named Bollman (if I remember right) were the only ones who defeated me in my efforts to learn something about them from their own lips.

The tobacco was best Virginia plug, worth about one dollar per pound (about three thousand dollars' worth). This little yawl (with a dirty sail), worth about twenty or thirty dollars, was earning two hundred dollars in one night in carrying Smith and his tobacco over.

As I said before, the Potomac was patrolled by gunboats, and the north shore was garrisoned at many points with troops, yet these little fellows would creep right in between them. My plan was to go equipped as they were, and meet them on their level.

We did not consider the neck between the Potomac and the Rappahannock as the enemy's country, yet the Confederates had a signal station on the Potomac all through the war; it was in charge of Harry Brogden, whom I knew. When I get along in my stories to June 30th, I will show you how well it was understood in the Confederacy.

Potomac Flotilla

To save delay in getting out of the harbour the following request was made:

> Headquarters, Middle Department,
> 8th Army Corps,
> Baltimore, June 9, 1864.

Capt. Cornell,
    Commanding Revenue Cutter,
    Baltimore Harbor.
Captain.—I have the honour to request that you permit the schooner *W. H. Travers* under command of Lieut. Smith, to pass your vessel without Custom Clearance. She is employed in the Secret Service Bureau, 8th A.C.

> Respy, your most obdt. servt.,
> John Woolley,
> Lt. Col. and Provost Marshal.

> Headquarters, Middle Department,
> 8th Army Corps.
> Baltimore, June 9, 1864.

Special Order No. 76.
Lieut. H. B. Smith with detachment of Secret Service Corps, will proceed on schooner *W. H. Travers* to such points on Eastern and Western shore of Maryland, Eastern and Western shore of Virginia, and Southern and Northern shore of the Potomac River, as he deems proper and necessary to further the instructions of the Government.

> By command of Major General Wallace,
> John Woolley, Lt. Col. and Provost Marshal.

The chain of war vessels extending along the Potomac under the command of Commodore Foxhall A. Parker, he having jurisdiction of the waters, was known as the Potomac flotilla.

When I attempted to approach the Commodore on his flag ship I was, in my raiment, a sight. The marines viewed me with curiosity. Upon introducing myself to the Commodore, he laughed. His wife being present, also enjoyed a laugh at my appearance. No "Johnny" ever looked more dilapidated. I presented my orders for the Commodore's endorsement.

Headquarters, Cavalry Detachment,
District of St. Mary's.
Leonardtown, Md., June 16, 1864.

Lieut. H. B. Smith,
    Chief Detective on board
       schooner *W. H. Travers.*

Some of my scouts last night arrested two men in a boat at the head of Britton's Bay, who claim to be Government detectives, and under your charge. If such is the case I desire that you will in some manner identify them, as they have nothing with them which would lead me to suppose them to be such.

These men give their names as John Gillock, and J. W. Lewis.

I shall hold these men in confinement until I am fully satisfied of the truth of their statements.

I am, Sir, very respy, yours, &c.,
F. W. Dickerson,
Lt. Comdg.

These were our boys and they were set at liberty of course. The Lieutenant was doing perfectly right, as our appearance and conduct was suspicious. Our plans always were to appear to be blockade-runners, so we never carried on our persons any evidence of our true character.

We carried forged Confederate documents when we were going where it was desirable. We could imitate General Winder's signature to passes, defying detection, and we had the same kind of paper, a light brown. The Confederate Government had poor stationery.

Headquarters, Middle Department,
8th Army Corps.
Baltimore, June 23, 1864.

Col. Woolley,
Provost Marshal.

Colonel.—I have the honour to report the following on the trip on the schooner *W. H. Travers* down the Bay, and on the Potomac River. I seized about three boxes tobacco (three hundred dollars) on the farm of Mr. Evans, Smith's Creek, St. Mary's County, Md, which he said was placed in his hay stack by some blockade runners.

I got from the Provost Marshal at Leonardtown, St. Mary's County, the canoe which was seized by Detective White sometime since.

In the Wicomico River, near its mouth, we seized a small yawl containing five men and one woman, who were on their way to Virginia. Wm. H. Hayden owned the boat and was to receive fifty dollars each for conveying the passengers over; he is engaged in this business constantly. About one week since he carried over two persons, one a Doctor; they were in the woods a day or so before they started.

Hayden has been carrying a mail to and fro. A small package of letters with a stone attached was found in the boat and I presume they were in Mr. Hayden's charge, as in the letters Mr. Hayden is mentioned as "carrying letters."

Wm. R. Horton, a passenger, was formerly in the Confederate army; said he was going to return; says he applied in this office for a position a short time since.

Wm. Gellatly and wife, passengers, were making their way to Columbia, S. C., Mr. Gellatly says he came within our lines early in April last, but did not report to any Provost Marshal, as he did not wish to bind himself not to return. He claims to be a British subject. They had a small trunk and some other baggage. Both Gellatly and Horton say that they made arrangements with Hayden in Chaptico, St. Mary's County.

I found in the trunk a small revolver. This arrest was made by Detectives Horner and Stern, who were posted as a picket near the mouth of the Wicomico.

There were two more men in the boat who succeeded in making their escape in the dark, and whom all the other passengers state were Confederate officers who had escaped from Point Lookout, named Bruce and Howell. I am informed that one of these parties left his horse with a Mr. Dent in Chaptico.

The yawl boat in which they were was very poor, worth about five or six dollars, and I did not bring it to Baltimore as it was not worth towing.

I took from Mr. Hayden a small gold watch. I also arrested Mr. J. B. McWilliams on the charge of aiding Rebels, contraband traders, &c., and of defrauding the Government. All of which I will state in a separate report.

On the trip we have laboured under many disadvantages. The vessel is in no way fit for the business, being too large and a miserable sailer. We could not get about as we ought, we had but one day's fair wind during the whole trip. We started from Wicomico River on Sunday at 3 p. m., and arrived in Baltimore this p. m. Mrs. Gellatly states that she tried to persuade her husband to remain North but he would not and she was compelled to accompany him. She came to this country about six months since.

I could not get permission from Commodore Parker to enter Virginia on account of the raid then being carried on, but he said under any other circumstances he would give permission and let a gunboat accompany me.

Hoping that my action in these matters will meet with your approval,

> I am, Colonel,
>> Very respy. your obdt. servt.,
>>> H. B. Smith,
>>>> Lt. and Chief.

Office Provost Marshal,
Baltimore, June 24, 1864.

Col. Woolley,
  Provost Marshal.

Colonel.—I have the honour to make the following report in the case of J. B. McWilliams of Charles County, Md., whom I arrested and brought to this prison.

While anchored in the Wicomico River on the trip down on the schooner *W. H. Travers*, W. H. Seward and myself took a small yawl which we had captured from Wm. H. Hayden in attempting to go South, and rowed up the Potomac River as far as Cobb Creek. We were hailed by McWilliams as we neared the shore at this point, he saying, "I used to own that boat," asked us where we were from. I refused to answer, but he said, "I am all right, you need not fear me." We landed and went up into the bushes. He advised us to remove the mufflers from the oars as they could be seen from the gunboats and they would know immediately that we were from Virginia. He informed us where the soldiers were posted and how to avoid them, and advised us to leave our boat on his shore as it was known and would not be suspected, informed us of Grant's move on Fort Darling, &c.; called our attention to an article in the *Baltimore Gazette* which he said "done him good," and would do any Southerner good.

He said he wanted to send some copies to Virginia as he knew they would be so highly appreciated; wanted to write by us to his son who was in the Confederate army; said he traded yawl boat with Hayden about one week previous, when Hayden was on his way to Virginia with two men, one of them a Doctor; said he talked with these two men nearly all one day, and sent a letter to his son by Hayden. He had sent his son a large revolver and wanted to sell me a double barrelled gun to take back with me to Virginia; said he had a full set of cavalry accoutrements that he had been keeping, awaiting a chance to saddle up and fight the Yankees.

He said he saddled his horse and started for Frederick to assist when Jackson made his first raid but he could not get through the lines. He said many times that the people of Maryland only wanted a chance to turn on the Yankees. He said Dr. Coon of Washington had a yacht in which he carried over as many as three hundred to join the Confederates, from near his place; he said he was much afraid of his negroes as they would go and tell the Yanks all that was going on; he advised me to watch the negroes especially on Sunday and advised us to scatter about the woods.

He brought us three meals in the woods. He whipped one of his negroes because he threatened to inform the Provost Marshal that we were there; he suggested to me the idea to lash one of his negroes down and carry him to Virginia; he said there were but four or five loyal men in the County.

Said he was caught once by the Yankee gunboats and they found seventeen thousand dollars worth of contraband goods in his cellar, but that he had a frolic at his house, invited all the ladies about there and the Officers of the gunboats and thus this was all hushed up; said he could bribe any Yankee.

He said at one time he stored $25,000 worth of contraband goods in his buildings and aided in getting them away but was not caught.

He said that about three weeks since, two Confederate soldiers, came across the river and secreted themselves in the woods; he went to see them; one of his slaves reported the case to the Provost Marshal, who sent a guard to make the arrest. He saw the guard approach. The Confederates were scared; he told them to keep cool and when the guards came near to say they wanted to know where the Provost Marshal was, to say they were refugees and wanted to take the oath; said he came near being caught but the Yanks were not smart enough; said he thought these men had returned to Dixie by this time.

He said the Government had attempted to confiscate his son Frank's one-third interest in some property there which was worth about ten thousand dollars, so he got Mr. Higgs, Post Master at Newport, Charles County, to make out an account against Frank amounting to about ten thousand dollars and sue the estate; he went security to pay the amount in five years and thus got the property in his hands.

I seized from his house the double barrelled gun and the horse equipments.

I arrested Mr. McWilliams and brought him to this city as I thought him too dangerous a man to occupy the position he does on the Maryland shore. His remarks were made voluntarily without my making much effort, apparently, to ascertain his actions.

> I am, Colonel,
>> Very respy. your obdt. servt.,
>>> H. B. Smith,
>>>> Lt. & Chief.

I remember the following incident which occurred on this trip: I tried to qualify as a deck hand. Leaning over the vessel's waist, I tried the difficult trick of scooping up a pail of water while the boat was in motion, and while so engaged my watch slipped out of my pocket, and into the water. We were then just below Fort Carroll, mid-stream. The watch is there yet, unless some mermaid has carried it off. I would not have lost it had I not divested it of the chain, to help appearances. On these trips one could not discover that we were not ordinary helpers "before the mast."

Many of the crews on such vessels were of the class called by the negroes "poor white trash," and they were ignorant beyond belief; to test which I once pointed out land to the east as being Ireland, to which they assented. The captains and mates, of course, were not so ignorant.

A strange picture presented itself to me one moonlight night. We were laying in St. Mary's River when a *cunna* (canoe) came along side, and three or four black men crawled upon our deck and hid themselves down behind the boat's waist. They wanted to go away with us, telling a pitiful tale of oppression, but slavery was yet in vogue there, and so we forced them to go away home.

FILE 16

Captain Bailey Makes a Capture

The following report was of another capture, by Captain Bailey:

Headquarters, Middle Department,
8th Army Corps.
Baltimore, June 29, 1864.

Col. Woolley,
Provost Marshal.

Colonel.—I have the honour to report that Capt. Wm. Bailey returned to this city this morning bringing three prisoners, and their skiff. They were first seen near James Point, and afterwards were taken on board the schooner *Thos. H. Northern*, Capt. Wells; from which schooner Bailey took them along with Capt. Wells, and brought them to this office. I had a conversation with each one separately and then confined them.

George Hull stated that he was in the 9th Virginia Cavalry, from which he deserted some three months since; that he has been in the Confederacy since 1862; that he ran the blockade into Virginia on the schooner *Sarah Elizabeth* from Philadelphia, loaded with an assorted cargo, and landed in the Rappahannock River; that he did not know he was going to run the blockade when he started. A man named Edwards, commanded the schooner.

Nicholas McKee states that he was a member of the Home Guards in King and Queen County, Virginia. He went into the Confederacy by the same vessel and at the same time with Hull, but did not know she was to run the blockade when she started. Neither Hull or McKee know who loaded the schooner; both deny all knowledge of their destination when they left Philadelphia.

Samuel Lewis was a member of the 9th Cavalry, Virginia. He states that he ran the blockade about June or July, 1863. He sailed from New York on a sloop with fifteen or twenty barrels of whiskey on board. They anchored under Ragged Point, Virginia, on the Potomac River, where they unloaded the whiskey. For some reason the men on the sloop got frightened and left him on the beach. He does not know the name of the sloop nor the name of the Captain, nor any person on board, and he, like the other two, did not know that the vessel intended to run the blockade.

It seems strange that none of them knew their destination when they shipped, and it also seems strange that after sailing from New York to the Potomac River, Wells had not learned the name of the vessel which he was on, or the names of any of his companions. He states also that he was the man sent ashore in Virginia, to do the business, but says he had to do it as it was orders from his Captain.

I have sent two detectives to see the schooner on which they were found, and to examine the cargo as it is discharged.

I am, Colonel,

Very respy. your obdt. servt.,

H. B. Smith,

Lt. & Chief.

The following letter to Mr. Plyle, introducing me as Mr. Shaffer, was the commencement of negotiations for the purchase of a lot of Confederate bonds, which purchase was consummated in the following November. For an account of which please refer to my report of the arrest of Brewer and Pittman, November 24th.

Baltimore, June 30, 1864.

Mr. Plyle.

Sir.—I expect to go to Norfolk or Richmond today. I send my partner, Mr. Shaffer, who will hand you this, to talk with you about purchasing your bonds. He will answer as well as I in the matter.

I will be back about July 10th.

Yours respy.,

Sinclair.

To Col. Plyle,
Franklin House.

A Confederate Letter

The following discloses how perfectly the Confederate government understood the travelled route through the lines. It was by way of their signal station on the Potomac, that was their official channel. I was determined to break it up.

Westmorland and Northumberland counties, Virginia, are the south shore of the Potomac River. Mosby, or at least part of his command, covered this country.

Confederate States of America,
War Department, Ordnance Bureau,
Richmond, June 30, 1864.

Captain:

The bearer, Mr. White, is confided in as trustworthy. He desires information as to the best mode of proceeding to Maryland.

I will thank you to give him any assistance you can consistently.

Mr. W. is engaged in procuring stores for the Government, through the blockade.

Very respy. your obdt. servt.,

J. Gorgas, Col.
Chief of Ordnance.

To Capt. Barker,
        In charge Signal Corps.
Approved,
        By order,
J. A. Campbell,
        A. Sec. War.
July 1, 1864.

This has endorsed on it:

Signal Bureau,
Richmond, July 1, 1864.

The officers in charge of Signal Station on Potomac, will furnish Mr. White any assistance in their power, in crossing into Maryland.

Wm. M. Barker,
Capt. in ch. Signal Corps.

The Ishmael Day Episode

About this time our efforts were pointed in another direction, for a portion of Lee's Army had been detached and had begun the invasion of Maryland (June 28, 1864).

General Wallace gathered up his scattered troops and prepared to meet the enemy at Monocacy. He was not well matched to meet them, but strongly resisted them long enough to enable Grant to reinforce Washington, and, strategically speaking, Wallace's fight saved Washington.

Appleton's Encyclopedia, page 130, under army operations 1864, says:

Meantime the enemy after tearing up some railroad from Frederick to Baltimore, sent their main body south of it and detached a cavalry force towards the Northern Central Railroad from Harrisburg, Pa., to Baltimore. This Cavalry expedition overran Maryland, 25 miles of the Northern Central Railroad was destroyed, and on Monday the 11th (July), a force appeared on the Baltimore, Wilmington & Phila. Road and captured and set on fire the trains at Magnolia station, seventeen miles south of Havre de Grace.

In one train Major General Franklin was captured but afterwards made his escape. Some damage was done to the track and Gunpowder Bridge was partially burned. The Cavalry heavily loaded with plunder came within six miles of Baltimore, then turning southward they joined the force near Washington which had been sent in that direction to guard against surprise; part of it halted before Fort Stevens on 17th street.

I remained in Baltimore until July 14th, when I started out to scout the country east and north of the city.

Headquarters, Middle Department,
8th Army Corps.
Baltimore, July 14, 1864.

Pass H. B. Smith and George W. Thompson on Department business out and in Picket Lines at all hours.

By command Major General Wallace.

John Woolley,
Lt. Col. & Pro. Marshal.

General Wallace had been compelled (by Lee's invasion) to take away to Monocacy nearly all of his troops, and so we had to appeal to the citizens for the defence of the city. All loyal citizens were appealed to and they responded nobly; they made, however, a motley army, but patriotic to the core, they vigorously performed their duty.

I had a serious experience with them when I tried to get inside our picket lines. We scoured the country quite thoroughly.

I find among my papers no copy of a written report except the one I find endorsed on and in connection with the report on Judge Grason's arrest on July 24th, which is the following:

When Bradley Johnson's Brigade, and Harry Gilmor's Cavalry was in Maryland, and after they destroyed the Gunpowder Bridge on the Philadelphia, Wilmington and Baltimore Railroad, one of my detectives named Thompson and myself went out past the Pickets on the Philadelphia Pike as far as the Rechabite Church and then changed onto the Belair road, where I hailed a man named —— ——, who was afterwards caught with a wagon loaded with contraband goods intended for the Rebs. He talked to me for some time. I told him that I wanted to get to see Harry Gilmor, that I was from New York, and that if Gilmor remained long enough in Maryland, I could get some recruits from New York.

This man offered me money to aid me in this glorious enterprise. He told me that if I would go over to Towsontown and see Richard Grason, that he (Grason) could tell me just where Gilmor could be seen. This man also told me about the man that Ishmael Day shot.

We left him and went over to Towsontown, where we had dinner and then went into Baltimore, after being arrested by (our) pickets almost every mile.

That evening we again started out for Towsontown; at Govanstown we were surrounded by about ten or twelve of the 13th Md., who lowered their pieces at us and demanded us to dismount; Thompson did so immediately, but I used more time. They said they had been waiting for us for some time. This of course was an error; finally we were released and proceeded on our way. We could not find Grason.

On our way back we were again arrested by some of the Citizen Cavalry, but got back into Baltimore at about 2 a. m.

(From the Baltimore *American*, July 12, 1864.)

Major Harry Gilmor, who, from a misguided leniency, if not something worse, was released from capture by General Wool, during his administration of affairs in this Department, was the commander of the Rebels who have worked so much destruction of property in this immediate vicinity.

After his successful plundering operations in Carroll and Frederick Counties he concluded to visit his own county and receive the congratulations of his friends and admirers. On Sunday he spent the day and evening at Glen Ellen, above Towsontown, at the residence of his father, Mr. Robert Gilmor, and no doubt a very pleasant time was had.

A force of about three hundred of his companions are said to have been encamped in that vicinity. On Sunday a delegation of five visited Towsontown and the joy of the Rebel males and females of that neighborhood is said to be beyond description. Mr. Richard Grason who frequently performs the office of special Judge of the County, was unable to restrain his emotion and kindly feelings to his friends, and took them to his dwelling where they feasted and whiskeyed to their hearts content.

Judge Grason in trying to escape arrest for his disloyal acts in connection with Harry Gilmor, tried to use a stolen pass issued to an assumed name, "Jenkins." I remember well my lecture to him on the heinousness of his offence. It was picturesque, a boy chiding a judge. But it was due him.

Headquarters, Middle Department,
8th Army Corps. Baltimore, July 24, 1864.

Lieut. Col. Woolley,
    Provost Marshal.
Colonel.—I have the honour to report the arrest yesterday of

Judge Grason of Towsontown.

I questioned him; he stated that a good friend of his whose name he refused to give, procured a blank pass and he filled in the name, residence and destination and attempted to pass on it.

I asked him the reason for assuming the name "Jenkins." He said he understood he was to be arrested and did not want to be detained. He said he received a letter from his home (near Queenstown), stating that his father was very poorly, and wanted to see him.

I asked him where the letter was. He said he threw it in the stove and burned it up. I asked if it was in his kitchen stove at home. He said no, that it was in his office stove. I asked him if he had a fire in his office stove (July). He said no, but that he set fire to the letter from his pipe that he was smoking.

He said he first heard he was to be arrested about the 11th, or 12th inst., and acknowledged to having kept out of the way as he did not want to be arrested then, as it would be some time, probably, before he could get a hearing, on account of the pressure of business on the Military Authorities.

He is everywhere known as being a bitter Rebel. He acknowledged to have spoken to Harry Gilmor while in Towsontown, but said it was only to get him to save some property.

He said he would rather receive the punishment than to allow the friend who gave him the pass to be punished.

I am, Colonel,

Very respy. your obdt. servt,

H. B. Smith,

Lt. & Chief.

The Ishmael Day incident was quite as romantic, or dramatic, as the "Barbara Freitchie" episode, but it was never dwelt upon, however, by the poets, nor can it be demolished as a myth. Ishmael Day, single handed and alone, defended his little miniature flag against the Confederate hosts. The incident rang over the country through the press.

My uncle, Zoeth Smith, a patriot indeed, wrote me to get Ishmael's picture, which I did. Recently, in looking over my papers, I found Uncle Zoe's letter and sent it to his sons, Truman and Addison, to show them the manner of man their father was when loyalty was needed.

The following appeared in the newspapers:

Ishmael Day

We had the pleasure this morning of an interview with Mr. Ishmael Day who yesterday morning shot down one of Harry Gilmor's men whilst in the act of taking down the flag over his gate in Harford County. He gives the following correct statement:

'On Sunday night he had heard that a party of Rebels were encamped in the vicinity, but did not give credence to the report. Early on Monday morning one of his negroes reported to him that they were coming down the road. He immediately hoisted his flag over the gate, and shortly after, two armed men came riding along the road and one seeing the flag burst out with a loud laugh, one of them advancing and seizing the halliards.

'The old gentleman, who is nearly seventy-three years of age, ran back into the house, threatening to shoot them if they did not desist. They paid no attention to him, but the halliards being twisted they had some difficulty in getting it down. By this time he had reached his second story, where his guns were, and raising the window fired a load from his duck gun just as the miscreant had succeeded in getting hold of the flag, and he fell back on the road seriously, and he thinks, mortally wounded, the whole load having entered his breast.

'Seizing another gun and a loaded Colt's revolver, he came down stairs and endeavoured to get a shot at the other, but he had run up the road. He then, in his anger, levelled at the wounded man, but he begged for mercy, and said he surrendered, and Mr. Day, thinking that he would never be able to haul down another flag, left him lying on the road.

'Hearing the approach of a large squad Mr. Day escaped with his weapons to the woods and eluded their pursuit. Mrs. Day was still in the house when the Rebels came up, and they immediately commenced to set fire to it after plundering it of such articles as they took a fancy to, and then set fire to it as well as his barn, which were entirely destroyed. They did not allow Mrs. Day to save even her clothing, and he fears that some two thousand, three hundred dollars of Government Bonds were destroyed with his deeds and papers. He has not yet seen Mrs. Day, who found refuge for herself and family in one of the neighbour's houses.

'The only regret of the gallant old patriot is that he did not get a shot at the other Rebel.'

We learn this morning that the man who was shot by Mr. Day was named Fields, formerly of Baltimore; that he was left by the Rebels at Dampman's Hotel, fifteen miles from the city on the Belair Road.

After the Confederates retreated I made a thorough examination into the disloyal conduct of various persons residing east and north of Baltimore, for the purpose, more particularly, to guide us in the future. The following is my report:

> Headquarters, Middle Department,
> 8th Army Corps.
> Baltimore, Aug. 7, 1864.

Lt. Col. Woolley,
 Provost Marshal.
Colonel.—I have the honour to report the connection of the following named persons with the Rebel raiders.
Herewith I hand you a transcript of the evidence in each case. No arrests have been made in these cases.
 I am, Colonel,
  Very respy. your obdt. servt.,
   H. B. Smith,
List of Names: Lt. & Chief.

Andrew Gill,	Henry Balton,
Stephen Gill,	Mal Guyton,
Charles Alden,	Wm. Price,
Jackson Dorney,	Henry Wesley,
J. Berryman,	John Y. Day,
—— Harriman,	S. Berryman,
—— Jones, Benj.	Worthington,
Francis Shipley,	Samuel Stone,
Chas. Shipley,	Jas. Reynolds,
John T. Johns,	—— Walker,
Henry Walker,	Mat. Shorman,
Murray Gill,	Marion Guyton,
Wm. Gore,	David Gittings,
Ed. Storm,	Henry Emmick,
Robert Elder,	Wm. Lowrey
—— Smith,	John Grovner,
Jos. Scarborough,	Jas. Mannon,
Wm. Knight,	Miss Lizzie Grason.

Trip to New York Regarding One Thomas H. Gordon

.

Headquarters, Middle Department,
8th Army Corps.
Baltimore, Aug. 13, 1864.

Special Order No. 111.

1st Lieut. H. B. Smith, Commanding Detective Corps, 8th Army Corps, will proceed to New York on business connected with this office. After completing his search and investigation he will return to these headquarters without delay.

Quartermasters will furnish transportation.

By command of Major General Wallace.

John Woolley,
Lt. Col. & Pro. Marshal.

The following is the report of the case I went to New York about:

Headquarters, Middle Department,
8th Army Corps.
Baltimore, Aug. 24, 1864.

Lt. Col. Woolley,
Provost Marshal.

Colonel.—I have the honour to report the following in the case of Thomas H. Gordon, paymaster.

I have on your order procured the check book ordered by him. Mess. Hoen & Co. say they have written to Nashville and Washington but have had no reply.

I also hand you two letters, one from Gordon and one from

Galloway, both in the same handwriting, as you will see on close examination.

Gordon represents himself as Captain.

The checks are entirely different from the usual paymaster's checks that are furnished by the United States depository.

I am, Colonel,

Very respy. your obdt. servt.,

H. B. Smith,

Lt. & Chief.

Dr. E. Powell, of Richmond

As our work progressed, we accumulated from Confederate mail, refugees and deserters, a mass of information as to the disloyalty of persons, which was carefully tabulated in a pigeonhole cabinet; we were constantly referring to it.

Headquarters, Middle Department,
8th Army Corps.
Baltimore, Aug. 17, 1864.

Col. Woolley:

I have information that a Thomas Bennett, U. S. mail carrier between Princess Ann and Newtown is in the Confederate service and is engaged to carry letters, &c., for them.

Let Smith put a sharp detective after him. Mr. E. J. Smith will talk with you about it.

Lew Wallace,
Major General Commanding.

War Department,
Washington, Sept. 16, 1864.

Memo.

Mr. J. P. Gulick, policeman at the Capitol grounds, gives information to the Department that Samuel Miles, a wholesale forwarding merchant in Baltimore, has been engaged in sending goods to the South.

Mr. Gulick lived at Wicomico Creek for some time during the war and while there observed the transaction, the goods coming to that point direct from Miles, and being from there run over into Little River by Samuel Langford, Miles's nephew.

The following is a Confederate letter addressed to Samuel G. Miles, referred to by Mr. Gulick. Miles was a merchant in high standing commercially. The letter is reproduced literally:

Monticello, Va.,
Feby. 29, 1864.

Mr. Miles.

Sir.—I take this privaledge to write to you asking the favour of you to send me by the gentleman that may hand you this letter to send me a few articles, you are well aware of our condition as to getting grocerys or a great many other things. Mr. Miles you will confer a great favour upon me to let me have a barril of sugar, one bag of coffee, 5 lbs. of tea, 15 gal. of Rye Whiskey. I would have sent money but you know that our money would not be of any survace to you. But if you send the above articles whether I get them or no you shall certainly be paid.

I was very sorry that I could not see you when you pass through to Richmond, as it would have afforded me great pleasure to have you at my house.

Give my respects to Mr. Langford and all enquiring friends. If it is not in your power to send the above name articles you will do me the favour to present this letter to Mr. Thomas Lumking and perhaps he may send them. By so doing you will oblige,

Your Friend,
Henry D. Barrick.

To
Mr. Samuel G. Miles.

The quantity of rye whiskey, compared to the other articles seemed pretty large. It reminds me of the story of the sloop captain who sent his man for supplies for a trip. The man brought two loaves of bread and a gallon of whiskey, at which the captain growled out "what made you buy so much bread?"

And here is another Confederate letter:

Richmond, Va.,
Oct. 24, 1864.

Mr. Steele.

Dear Sir.—I have been waiting very anxiously to hear if you had succeeded in making the arrangements with Allison to take us to Baltimore.

If it is possible to get Allison or any other person with a schooner to make the trip to Baltimore and bring back goods, make the arrangement for the trip and let me know when I am to come down and I will come prepared to make the trip.

Any goods you may wish to bring I will take through in my name. Let me hear from you as soon as you can hear from Allison.

Your obdt. servant,

Dr. E. Powell.

Cor. Main & 10th Sts.,
    Richmond, Va.

Terrence R. Quinn

Terrence R. Quinn, previously spoken of, backed by his military friends, complained of abuse which he alleged was put upon him by our officers, and I was called upon to make the following statement in reply:

> Office Provost Marshal,
> Baltimore, Md.,
> Oct. 20, 1864.

Lt. Col. Woolley,
  Provost Marshal.
Colonel.—I have the honour to make the following statement regarding the arrest of Terrence R. Quinn, and the causes for such arrest.

On or about March 18, 1864, I arrested Quinn by order of Major H. Z. Hayner, then Provost Marshal of this Department.

This arrest was caused by statements made by one John W. Lewis, to the effect that during a period of six or eight months then last past, at different times Quinn had stated to him that he was engaged in running the blockade and held out great inducements for Lewis to join him. He (Quinn) stating that he was the owner of several schooners, and told how he got clear on a former charge of the same kind, at the same time admitting his guilt.

On searching Quinn's house, No. 23 Constitution street, I found a great many letters addressed to parties in Richmond, Confederate officers and others, which were letters of introduction, stating that it was Mr. Terrence R. Quinn's intention to visit Richmond and recommending him as "always a friend of the South."

These letters were written by Rebel officers in confinement at Fort McHenry. There were also other letters showing that Quinn had aided in defrauding the government out of some bonds, and letters corroborating Quinn's statements in regard to contraband trade. All of these letters were given to Major Hayner.

On arresting Quinn I took him in a carriage to Vineyard Hotel, as it was deemed proper to keep him closely confined until I could have time to go to the Eastern shore of Va., and seize his schooners.

He was given a fine room at this hotel and his expenses, about seventeen dollars per week were all paid by me. He was placed under a Military guard, and was afterwards transferred to the prison attached to this office, for examination by an officer sent here by the Secretary of War.

On seizing Quinn's schooners I found Capt. J. J. Lewis in command of one.

This Lewis was formerly arrested and confined in Fort McHenry on a charge of blockade running.

He admitted his guilt to me but stated that he was released without a trial. He is a specimen of the characters in Quinn's employ.

In 1862 Quinn was arrested on charge of blockade running but was released without trial. He stated to Lewis that he was guilty but the government was not smart enough to prove it.

I again caused the arrest of Quinn on Sept. 8, 1864, on an order from General Stevenson, commanding at Harper's Ferry, on the charge of running negroes away from Va., on forged passes. General Stevenson also ordered search for passes. I also caused the arrest of a negro named Andrew Jackson, who stated that Quinn tried to get him in the army as a substitute, and also that he did not go to the Provost Marshal for a pass but that Quinn sent another negro.

As to his being treated brutally: When arrested he was intoxicated, and two or three times called the officers names, whereupon the officers struck him, once only. My first acquaintance with Quinn was when I was Assistant Provost Marshal at Fort McHenry.

He claims that he is a British subject and not amenable to our laws.

I am, Colonel,

Very respy. your obdt. servt,

H. B. Smith,

Lt. & Chief.

Arrest of Ferry, Donohue and Newcomb

The Presidential election of 1864 was then upon us, and indeed it was most momentous. The issue was to determine the life of this Union. Mr. Lincoln was renominated, and General George B. McClellan was nominated to run against him. And quite fittingly, Horatio Seymour, who was to have been leader of secession in the North (according to my information), who had lent his whole influence towards obstruction, was made chairman of the convention that nominated McClellan.

A resolution of the convention read:

Resolved, that this Convention does explicitly declare, as the sense of the American people, that after four years of failure to restore the Union by experiment of War . . . the public welfare demands that immediate efforts be made for a cessation of hostilities.

In the convention Mr. Wickliffe, of Kentucky, said:

The delegates from the West were of the opinion that circumstances may occur between noon of today and the 4th of March next (inauguration day) which will make it proper for the Democracy of the Country to meet in Convention again.

What could he have referred to? Solve the riddle if you can. Ponder on a "Northwestern Confederacy"; the Sons of Liberty, and the seizure of their arms; and also on Lincoln's assassination, only a few days after March 4th, 1865.

All of this leads me to what I am about to tell about that election, wherein the same influences that failed with bullets to disrupt the

Union were now trying to accomplish the same purpose with ballots.

I will not charge McClellan with disloyalty, yet I cannot help asking why did he lend his name to the disloyal movement? There were disloyal Northerners, but not one of them voted for Lincoln.

I do not claim that all who voted for McClellan were disloyal, but that all the disloyal, including all blockade-runners and bounty jumpers, voted for him.

On the 21st of April, 1864, a law was enacted in New York State called "an act to enable the qualified electors of this State, absent therefrom in the military service of the United States, in the Army or navy thereof, to vote."

This law provided for a power of attorney appointing a proxy who would present his (the soldier's) sealed envelope, addressed to the election inspectors in his home or residence district. The ballot was to be in a sealed envelope, and to be opened only by the inspectors; this envelope was to be enclosed in another, outer envelope addressed to his proxy. The outer envelope was to contain also the power of attorney for the proxy to so present the sealed ballot.

And now I will tell you how merely the misplacing of the letter "L" betrayed one of the greatest crimes of the period, entirely defeated its perpetration, and helped to save our Union.

On Thursday afternoon, October 20th, 1864, General Wallace came to my office with Mr. Orville K. Wood, of Clinton county, New York.

Mr. Wood had a blank or partly blank document which he had found in possession of a soldier from his county. It was a blank power of attorney, such as were provided for voting under the law of April 21st, 1864. The jurat was signed in blank:

C. G. Arthur

Lieut. 11th U. S. Cavl.

—and their conclusion was that this officer may have signed a number of such papers in blank, and passed them out, to be used by any soldier, perhaps to facilitate voting; an illegal act in itself; but upon examination I pronounced the officer's signature a forgery. My conclusion was based on the fact of the letter "l" in "Cavl." I assumed that no officer of cavalry, more especially in the regular service, would abbreviate in any way other than Cav. or Cavy.

General Wallace saw the force of my reasoning, and a new light was thrown on the matter.

Had the one letter "l" been absent I should have concluded as General Wallace and Mr. Wood had, *i. e.*, that the fact of such a document, entirely blank except the officer's jurat, being in public hands, was a wrong merely laying the officer liable for having attached his name to a blank paper.

The point then was to find out where the work was done. Mr. Wood had visited the New York State agency office in Fayette Street and I arranged for him to go there again the next morning (Friday), he to tell the representative, Mr. Ferry, that some friends would call to be assisted in preparing their votes. We agreed that my name would be "Phillip Brady," from West Chazy, Clinton County, New York.

Friday morning I equipped myself as became a private soldier, in a uniform much worn and shabby. One of my men, Mr. Babcock, accompanied me, he was similarly attired. We provided ourselves with "2 hour" passes from the Camden Street Hospital, and sicker looking convalescents never were seen outside of a hospital. When we arrived at Ferry's office we appeared much exhausted. Mr. Wood introduced me, and then I insisted on Mr. Ferry's reading my pass so that he would know exactly who I was; I told him I wanted to vote for Mr. Lincoln, because he was the soldier's friend.

He went in an adjoining room and brought out one of the same powers of attorney that Mr. Wood had shown me the day before, for me to sign; the jurat was executed and the ink was not yet dry on it. To give myself more time to examine, I hesitated in signing my name, I was so sickly (?) and weak, I had Mr. Ferry help guide my hand. I had by this time located Mr. "Arthur" in the next room.

Mr. Ferry then discovered he had no Lincoln ballots, but said he expected them from the printer. He volunteered, if I would leave it to him, to put in a proper ticket, and mail it for me, to which I consented. I told him I did not know when I might get another pass.

Ferry gave me a plug of tobacco and a pair of socks, to illustrate, I suppose, the Empire State's interest in her volunteers.

Babcock then went through the same process, which gave me all the time needed to survey the surroundings, whereupon we left.

Mr. Wood remained, but came out afterwards and met me by appointment, on Charles Street. He was startled at the condition of affairs in the State Agent's office, where a corps of men were engaged in forgery, and did not want to return there, but was persuaded to go back and put in the day. The character and magnitude of the crime prompted us to great secrecy.

Lucius F. Babcock

The next day (Saturday) General Wallace went to Washington. A Cabinet meeting was held to consider the election frauds.

Next morning (Sunday), the following order was issued by General Wallace, personally, and is in his handwriting:

> Headquarters, Middle Department,
> 8th Army Corps.
> Baltimore, Md., Oct. 23, 1864.

Lt. Col. John Woolley,
> Provost Marshal.

You will immediately arrest the following persons: M. J. Ferry, Ed. Donohue, Jr., and such clerks, assistants, &c., as they may have in the office of the New York State Agency in Baltimore. You will also seize and take into your possession all books, papers, letters, &c., which you may find on the persons or in the rooms and baggage of the persons above named.

The prisoners you will take to the City jail and confine them separately, allowing no visitor to have communication with or the prisoners to have communication in any manner with each other.

> Lew Wallace,
> Major General Commanding.

(You will also station a guard at the door of the office of said Agency. L. W.)

Upon my request to be allowed to conduct the arrests and seizures in my own way, the General ran a pen through the words that are bracketed.

It was my desire to kidnap the parties, so that warning might be given to other places, such as Washington, Harper's Ferry and City Point, to look out for similar crimes, to accomplish which it was desirable to leave behind each person, at his home or office, a reasonable excuse for his absence for a few days, and to keep the State Agency office open to callers.

I employed a hack and a confidential driver, one used to me, and who would carry out instructions to the letter.

With one of my men I drove to near the State Agency Office. We entered and were met by Donohue, who was alone (it was early Sunday a.m.) and was pugnacious when he was made aware of his dilemma. I arranged with him, that for friendly appearances, we would walk out arm in arm to our carriage. Then we were whisked away to my office. I left Mr. Kraft, one of my men, in the office to run it and tell callers that Donohue had "gone out."

I learned from Donohue that Ed. Newcomb was stopping at Barnum's hotel. At the hotel I found Newcomb's room number, went to it and rapped on the door. I informed him there was a party from New York at the office, and that Donohue wanted him at once; he accompanied me out the private entrance and into my carriage. After a while he remarked that the driver was not going right. I told him I was a stranger but I guessed the driver knew the way; finally I told him of his position, that he would meet Donohue, but not at the State Agency office.

When we came near our office I changed hats with him to prevent recognition. An Albany regiment, the 91st, was guarding our office- Newcomb was an Albany lawyer. I placed him in my office with Donohue, but with officers both inside and outside the door. I took his pocketbook, room-door key, and papers, and I returned to Barnum's to "put them to sleep."

Shawls were commonly used then, especially by Northerners. I searched his room, muffled myself up in his shawl, presented his key at the desk, asked for and paid his bill, putting the receipt in his pocketbook, and told them that Mr. Newcomb would stop over Sunday and a few days with friends, in case of inquiry. I handed Newcomb his pocketbook and baggage.

Meantime Mr. Kraft was running the State Agency office, answering callers all right.

The next move was to get Mr. Ferry, who resided in the far west end of the city. I drove out there accompanied by Mr. Babcock. Ferry had not returned from church (think of the moral tone of one who had forged all the week). On his return I told him there were important parties at his office from New York and that Donohue wanted him at once; he excused himself to the ladies and accompanied me in the carriage. The ride was long, so we visited in a friendly way, but finally he, too, remarked that the driver was going out of his way, and after protesting considerably, I informed him of his true status. He did not quite collapse. I assured him his years would earn him a gentleman's treatment. He was soon landed in my office.

I had a good dinner served all of them from my hotel. So that the ladies at Mr. Ferry's house would not worry, and waiting until it would have been impossible for them to reach the boat, I wrote them on his own letter head asking for clean clothes enough to last about a week, as he was going to City Point—so I wrote—on the Bay Line boat, on important business. The clean clothes I gave Mr. Ferry.

I then went back to the office to see how much business Mr. Kraft had accomplished. He was much warmed up over his discoveries in that room adjoining, where the forgeries were done.

While there a brusque, loud-mouthed man came in and asked for Donohue, announcing in a loud way what he had done at Harper's Ferry. I told him he was a fool, and that I would not have anything to do with the business if such as he were in it. The chiding acted like a charm. He thanked me for cautioning him. He said he would not have spoken so but he knew that I was all right. He said he was stopping at the Fountain House, but readily agreed to go and get his bag and go with me to my hotel; he accompanied me and landed where the others were. His name was Kerley, and if my memory is correct, he was running for sheriff of Washington county.

After dark, having prepared a separate corridor in the city jail, I placed them there, taking the following receipt:

Baltimore, Oct. 23, 1864.
Received of guards the following prisoners:
Edw. Donohue.
Edw. Newcomb.
M. J. Ferry.
Peter Kerley.
(Signed)   Thomas C. James, Warden.
John W. Sindall.

On Monday (24th) we had a conference with Mr. Fred. Seward, Assistant Secretary of State (he was accompanied by Mr. Benedict, of the State Department), to ascertain if some one of the batch would confess. I suggested Newcomb, and went in the carriage for him.

The city jail was in a gloomy location. The hour was well along in the evening, and Newcomb's nerve was shaky. I took him to the Eutaw House, before General Wallace, Colonel Woolley and Mr. Seward. At first he (Newcomb) stoutly denied knowledge of the forgeries; my judgment as to his probable weakness was in jeopardy. I asked Newcomb to come out in the hall, where I told him that he could do just as he saw fit about confessing, but that I was the convalescent soldier who voted right there in the office when Donohue and he were doing the work. Then he begged to be again taken before General Wallace, whereupon he confessed all.

In the meantime I had choked up the mail and express companies for all matter bearing the New York State Agency label, and among the mass we got my document, but it contained a good straight Mc-Clellan ballot, as did Mr. Babcock's.

On Tuesday (the 25th) the Doubleday Military Commission of Washington was convened at Baltimore, and before the day was over Newcomb had confessed and Ferry tried to, but he so falsified his statement that it did not merit consideration. The desirability for haste to make public the fraud was because the country had been flooded with these fraudulent papers, which could not be intercepted, except by publicity through the channel of the newspapers; therefore after the 27th of October the matter was made public.

Appleton says they were arrested on the 27th, but the facts, "between the lines," are as I have told you. The kidnapping was a success. Four public men were taken away from their business and usual haunts, and hidden for four days without leaving a trace.

I found in Ferry's office many rich things. Among them was a letter from Ferry to John F. Seymour, Hudson, Columbia County, New York (the Governor's brother), accompanying a package of these forged papers, and telling him to use them where his judgment suggested, or words to that effect.

I offered General Wallace to try to incriminate Seymour, if I could have two or three days' time; but the General advised against it, having so little time even then for publicity before election day.

The whole country was roused to action. The matter was treated by the newspapers as of as much importance as the army movements. It was given first column, first page, place, with flaming, startling headlines. One paper had it:

Great Soldier Vote Fraud. Arrest of Governor Seymour's State Agents. The Most Stupendous Fraud Ever Known in Politics."
"A systematic and widespread conspiracy has been brought to light, carried on by agents here (Washington), at Baltimore, Harper's Ferry and in the Army of the Potomac. Men now in custody have been actively engaged in this business for weeks, as one of the parties involved (Newcomb) declared. Forged ballots have been forwarded in dry goods boxes, etc.

Such startling accounts were continued for many days. It was also treated editorially. It was not considered merely as a political move to secure office, but as a move to secure a false verdict on the matter of the continuance of the war. *Appleton's Encyclopedia* for 1864 has several columns of matter on the election fraud case.

The following order was issued by Major General Hooker, commanding the Northern Department.

Cincinnati, Ohio.
Oct. 27, 1864.

The Commander of this Department has received information that it is the intention of a large body of men on the Northern frontier, on each side of the line, open on one side and in disguise on the other, to so organize at the ensuing National Election, as to interfere with the integrity of the election, and when in their power to cast illegal votes, &c."

A number of Ohio election officers were arrested for imitating the New York State Agents' rascalities.

Notwithstanding all efforts made to publish the facts, the conspirators came too near success. New York polled about 730,000 votes; Mr. Lincoln's majority was only about 6,700; and of the total vote of 2,401,000 in the great States of New York, Pennsylvania, Ohio, Indiana and Illinois, if less than three *per cent.* had been cast on the other side, Lincoln would have been defeated and the Union destroyed. A twig may change the trajectory of a cannon ball; a letter "I" misplaced, may have saved the nation.

Will any one conclude that Ferry, the State's Agent, and Donohue and Newcomb, were not acting under orders from their superior, Governor Seymour?

Just now while I am writing I have before me Watson's Magazine for March, 1911, speaking of Headley's account of his part in retaliatory acts in the west and east: "The evidence there found of the extent of the copperhead movement in the upper Mississippi Valley in 1863-1864 is entirely essential to a history of both sides of the great war. It becomes startling to contemplate to what imminence revolution in the States of the north and west had approached, etc."

Mr. Davis (Jefferson Davis) delivered an impassioned speech at Palmetto Station, near Atlanta, in Sept., 1864, in which he declared the opinion that McClellan would be elected over Lincoln at the November elections, and in that event the west would set him up as president over itself, leaving the east to Lincoln.

Thus it is shown that the Confederates fully expected a rupture of the North on lines to be worked out by the "Sons of Liberty" and their co-conspirators.

After a time President Lincoln pardoned Ferry and later Donohue. The President's big-heartedness led him first to pardon Ferry because of his advanced age.

Newcomb came into my life again in 1882, in the impeachment proceedings against Judge Westbrook. Somebody hunted me up and subpoenaed me to testify as to the character of Newcomb. He had been a receiver of a life insurance company (if my memory is right) under an appointment by Judge Westbrook, and it was represented that he had misapplied large sums. The session of the committee was held in the St. James Hotel, corner of Broadway and Twenty-sixth Street, New York. When I entered the rotunda I was hailed by a Mr. Fox, who wanted conversation with me. He knew my mission and told me it would be worth a thousand dollars if I would "walk up the street with him." The proposition did not flatter me; he did not correctly size up my moral tone. I testified concerning the circumstances of 1864, of Newcomb's crime and his confession. Newcomb followed me out of the committee room, and expressed great surprise at my appearance on the scene. I was not astonished to find him in questionable business.

Donohue I have met several times since the war. For a time he was in the employ of the New York Central Railroad, later holding a small political appointment in one of the New York City departments.

I found another document in the State Agent's office that finished Adjutant General Andrews' usefulness instanter. It was written on headquarters' letterhead and spoke disrespectfully of Mr. Lincoln, the commander-in-chief. Andrews was unceremoniously dismissed from the service.

John Deegan, a Forger, Captured

Here follows a rather interesting case. One Deegan, an expert pen-man, who had formerly been a clerk in one of the regular cavalry regiments, had been forging discharges and final statements of ficti-tious soldiers, employing an accomplice to present them at the various paymasters' offices and draw the money.

Being familiar with the officers' signatures, he was very success-ful in forging their names. To make the final statement cover a large amount of money—many hundreds and sometimes thousands of dol-lars—the statements represented the parties to have been prisoners of war, one or two years, which, with all the allowances, would carry the amounts up into large figures.

United States Army, Pay District
of Pennsylvania.
Baltimore, Md., Nov. 9, 1864

Colonel:

I have had a full explanatory conversation with your Chief of Detectives in reference to forgeries lately perpetrated upon the Government and have given him every clue in my possession, to the perpetrators.

The name and recent address of the party who escaped from your office has also been obtained by me. I have therefore to request that you give him every facility he may desire in visiting both Philadelphia and New York, and that you will instruct the calling to his assistance experienced detectives.

I have ordered my orderly to report to him as he is acquainted with this Deegan. The case is one of importance and no delay should occur in ferreting it out.

Very respy.
Colonel, your obdt. servant,
Frank M. Etting,
To   Chief Paymaster.
Lt. Col. Woolley,
Provost Marshal,
8th Army Corps.

Headquarters, Middle Department,
8th Army Corps.
Baltimore, Nov. 9, 1864.

Special Order No. 164.

Lt. H. B. Smith, 5th N. Y. H. Arty. and two men will proceed without delay to the cities of Philadelphia and New York, for the purpose of arresting certain persons engaged in manufacturing forged Discharge papers. Having accomplished this duty, Lieut. Smith and his guard will return and report at this office. The Quartermaster's Department will furnish the necessary transportation.

By command of Major General Lew Wallace.
Wm. H. Wiegel,
Capt. & Asst. Provost Marshal.

We had in custody one of Deegan's pals, John Battell. To save his scalp, I forced him to write a letter (copy below), that I might use with Deegan.

Deegan's Philadelphia address was a saloon, kept by Dick Callery, at 126 Callowhill Street. The letter reads:

Havre de Grace, Nov. 8th.

Wm. Deegan.

I am under arrest on my way to Baltimore under arrest I have just time through the goodness of a guard to send you this as we delayed here one ½ hour waiting for another train to pass it will go hard with me I suppose.

Yours,
John Battell.

The above is a literal copy of Battell's letter, it is in his handwriting and is addressed to:

Wm. Deegan, 11th Ward Hotel,
Private.   Callowhill St., Philadelphia, Pa.

We were attired suitably for the occasion, velveteen caps, paper collars, coloured shirts, etc., a good "jumper's" toggery.

Jumpers, or bounty jumpers, were a very distinct class of patriots (?) in war days. They were so patriotic they would enlist many, many times, and draw a large bounty each time. When they enlisted they doffed their clothes and put on the uniform. As soon as they could evade or "jump" the guards conducting them, they would shed the uniform and buy a cheap suit, such a one as I have described, and reappear at their old haunts, ready to "jump" another bounty, under the skilful management of a bounty broker. An observing person could pick out a "jumper" on sight.

We put in twenty-four lively hours with the "jumpers" and thieves at Callery's. One may wonder how a decent man could associate with such characters and not betray himself. It is a wonder, but somehow I managed to fit the niche under any circumstances.

Learning that Deegan had gone to New York and would probably be at his brother John's saloon in East 38th Street, I proceeded there.

I used the names "George Comings" or "I. K. Shaffer" usually, and they became familiar to me. In this case I was "George Comings."

To have something to recommend me to John Deegan, I wired to myself from Philadelphia to New York, using "R. Callery's" name (without permission), I have the telegram, which was done by the House Printing Telegraph (in type on long strips, or tape, much like the present ticker tape). It reads:

Phil Nov 11th

Geo Comings. Wm Deegan is at John Deegans Thirty Eighth Street Second and Third Avenues. Please take that note to him (Battell's note.)

Hund. twenty-six Callowhill St.

We associated with the "jumpers" who hung out at John Deegan's to accomplish our purposes. Wm. Deegan had gone to Boston.

Bounty jumpers in New York were on every corner. The city was infested with them. Our appearance and conduct secured us recognition by them, so much so that my men became anxious on account of our popularity.

I made arrangements with Major Leslie, the Chief Paymaster in New York, for the capture of Deegan, which was accomplished shortly afterwards. When I called on Major Leslie at his residence in 9th Street, I was somewhat shocked at first at his incivility. I had overlooked the fact that my personal appearance (my clothes, etc.) did not merit confidence. However, as soon as I made him know me everything went on all right. I must certainly have looked tough.

Headquarters, Middle Department,
8th Army Corps.
Baltimore, Nov. 15, 1864.

Lt. Col. Woolley,
Provost Marshal.

Colonel.—I have the honour to submit the following report of my trip to Philadelphia and New York, in search of William Deegan and others charged with forgeries.

Among other steps that Major Elting took, previous to giving the matter into my hands, was to telegraph the Provost Marshal at Philadelphia to visit certain places and arrest, if found, William Deegan.

I arrived in Philadelphia on Thursday morning and immediately called on the Provost Marshal to ascertain what steps he had taken, and I requested him to withdraw his men from the job.

I ascertained to a certainty that Deegan had gone to New York, and also that the officers from the Provost Marshal's office went there (to the haunt of Deegan), dressed in uniform, stating they were connected with the Quartermasters' Office, and wanted to see Deegan. This was sufficient to scare any guilty man out of the country; accordingly I left for New York, where I visited Deegan's haunts. On Friday evening there, I ascertained that Deegan and his pigeons were gone, either to New Jersey or Boston.

On Saturday I visited Major Leslie, Chief Paymaster at New York, and posted him as to the actions of Deegan and his associates, and recommended that if discharges purporting to come from the 6th United States Cavalry were presented it would be well to detain the parties presenting such discharges and final statements until he could ascertain if they were genuine; and would then probably be able to catch some of the pigeons, and perhaps Deegan. I also requested him to telegraph to Chief Paymaster at Boston, which he promised to do.

Deegan's forgeries seem to be confined to the 6th U. S. Cavalry; he was formerly a member of that Regiment. He operates with "jumpers."

I think this job was spoiled by the actions of the Officers in Philadelphia. I am quite positive we were not suspected, as we were at all times current with these "jumpers," that infested Deegan's haunts.

I visited these places until yesterday, when I became satisfied that Deegan is too badly scared to remain about.

In addition to my report I wish to give you a brief outline of the state of affairs in the Provost Department in New York and Philadelphia. Wherever I went in search of my man I met "Bounty Jumpers," who openly avowed themselves such, and seemed to defy the authorities. Dick Callery, who keeps a grog-gery at No. 126 Callowhill street, Philadelphia, stated he was aware of Deegan's transactions. Most of Callery's customers were "jumpers."

In New York we could go but a short distance without meet-ing these characters. From what I could see I should think one thousand a low estimate of their numbers; they are very bold. They pay this Department quite a compliment, *i. e.*, they say if they can only get clear from Baltimore they are all right.

If about fifteen or twenty pigeons could be thrown into New York and Philadelphia to co-operate with a strong force of De-tectives and Military, hundreds of these "jumpers" would be brought to justice.

These jumpers without an exception are the firm support and backbone of the Copperhead Clique, and the same parties that caused the riots in New York last year. The arrest and punish-ment of these parties would cause rejoicing among respectable people. From my observation I can see that this class of men before the war were pickpockets, burglars, &c., but now resort to this last and easier means of stealing, *i. e.*, "bounty jumping," at the same time they please the "Copperheads" by filling suc-cessively, the quotas of different districts, and not furnishing the Army one soldier; thus defeating the object of the Draft.

I am, Colonel,

Very respy. your obdt. servt.,

H. B. Smith,

Lt. & Chief.

My report and recommendations were so highly esteemed by General Wallace that he had a copy sent to General N. L. Jeffries, the

Provost Marshal General of the United States, and by him were my suggestions acted upon. Colonel Lafayette C. Baker was sent to New York with a force of men and very ample money; a very vigorous and extended raid was made, partially successful, but I think my plan of putting fifteen or twenty men in with the jumpers, to actually "jump" with them, thus obtaining evidence to convict, would have been more successful. The current newspapers treated this matter as of great importance, using the findings of my report, saying: "Our quotas are being fraudulently filled, and furnishing no men for the army, etc."

A Train Robbery, Paymasters Robbed

Coleman's Eutaw House,
Baltimore, Nov. 19, 1864.

(Unofficial.)

Hon. C. A. Dana,

Asst. Sec. of War.

Dear Sir.—Lt. Smith, my Chief of Detectives, will hand you this note.

It is necessary to one of his schemes, based upon a late discovery, that he should have a pass from the Secretary of the Navy to go through the lines of the blockade on the Potomac. The pass should cover a vessel, a crew of six or seven men and two or three hundred dollars' worth of goods.

I have every confidence that Lt. Smith will uncover a good thing.

About his honesty there is no doubt.

Very truly,

Your friend, Lew Wallace,

Major General Commanding.

The above letter is in General Wallace's own handwriting. I prize it more than any commission or brevet commission that I have.

I needed just such an extended privilege as General Wallace asked for, and in March following I obtained it.

Colonel John S. Mosby's Guerillas were the most annoying and expensive antagonists we had. He operated along the line of the Baltimore & Ohio Railroad west of Washington, and also with a detachment between the Potomac and Rappahannock. My probings extended into the territory covered by him. I made a study of his tactics and was preparing to counteract him. His men were at home in the district; it was, in fact, their home. They were, or many of them were, farmers, who might be innocently tilling the soil as our scouting parties passed, but who, at Colonel Mosby's whistle, if the chance was propitious, would jump on horse and surprise us before long. Small bodies of troops were taken unawares. They never offered a front to large bodies; they would swoop down on a defenceless train, or destroy railroad bridges.

Mosby was a valuable asset to the Confederacy, worth many times Harry Gilmor's Raiders.

I think, without doubt, it took twenty or thirty thousand of our men to guard against his intermittent incursions.

Mosby was an educated man. An impression was abroad then that he was a barbarian; he was not. He was loyally doing for the South what I would have done for the North. I captured his foraging order, on one occasion and it opened my eyes for it was evidence of as civilized methods of war as was ever manifested. In this order he provided for payment for private property which he took.

I planned to organize a body of men to compete with Mosby, and I asked for a command to operate independently of district lines, or military commanders.

I had been locating Mosby's men (their homes), from all sorts of sources of information, preparing to capture them in detail. I was planning to take them at their disadvantage, when they were at the plough, and not when they were in the saddle. Here is part of my list so tabulated:

MEMBERS OF MOSBY.

Wm. Robinson,

Wend Robinson,

John Robinson—Three miles above Front Royal, on the Culpepper Pike. Father is a farmer. Geo. Reger—Black Rock below the Pike, with his brother, John Reger.

Jack Downing—½ mile from Geo. Reger's on Black Rock, in a fine brick house.

William Wright—Four miles below Front Royal, on the Linden Road, with his Grandmother, Luanda Wright.

James Fold—Below Flint Hill, six or seven miles from Front Royal near the Pike. Father is a farmer.

James Hawes—On Culpepper Pike, seven miles from Front Royal, is a labourer, lives in Mr. Gibson's house.

Bresley Esom—Seven miles from Front Royal, one mile from Culpepper Pike.

George Esom—Same place as Bresley.

John Clark—Nine miles from Front Royal, to right of Culpepper Pike, on the mountain. Father is a farmer.

John Maddox—Four miles from Front Royal on Hominy Road, is a farmer.

George Leech—Three miles from Front Royal, on the Culpepper Pike. Shoemaker shop.

James Bolton—Eight or nine miles from Front Royal, on Culpepper Pike, left hand side. Father is a blacksmith.

James Anderson—Resides with Bolton.

William Blackwell—Formerly on Baltimore & Ohio Railroad.

You will see later on in Paine's statement that I quizzed him on the same subject. I presume my information was not always reliable, but was nearly so.

The following is quoted from an interrupted Confederate letter, in speaking of Mosby:

He is well off for Greenbacks since he captured those paymasters on the Baltimore & Ohio Railroad line. When the plunder secured on that occasion came to be divided up every officer and man who assisted got $1,922.50. A good deal of this money you have already got back. I will tell you how. Old men and women residents in the neighbourhood of Upperville, who have gone within your lines and taken the oath of allegiance, have been sent by Mosby and many of his men to Berlin, to purchase goods: such as hats, &c., and have paid for these in captured Greenbacks, and got the goods out to the Battalion.

This information was correct. I captured one man's part of the plunder entire, or nearly so. The money was yet in its original shape, as issued to these paymasters from the Treasury Department. I took it there and they were able to identify the packages.

The capture was made in this way: One of Mosby's men named Dr. John A. Kline, of Loudoun County, Virginia, came to Baltimore. He was accompanied by his mother, Mrs. Mary A. Kline, and a niece, Nannie O. Bannon. He became intoxicated, talked too much, and the whole party was arrested. They were searched, the women by one of my female officers, and the money, about two thousand dollars, was found on the mother, in a belt worn next to her skin. We confined the women in a hotel, but were finally forced to send them to jail, as the mother got intoxicated, and so disturbed the other guests.

Kline was sentenced to ten years hard labour. The mother was confined until the close of the war.

Appleton, for 1864, speaks of the train robbery, on page 156, as follows:

All that district of country west of Washington and immediately south of the Potomac River, was infested with guerrillas throughout the year. Colonel Mosby was their leader. Many of their expeditions were conducted with great boldness. Sometimes they came within a few miles of Washington.

On one occasion during the year they captured a passenger train on the Baltimore and Ohio Railroad, between Harper's Ferry and Martinsburg. A rail was removed, and the train thus running off the track was brought to a stop. Their proceedings have been thus graphically described, etc.

They then made a final search, and saw the work was complete; the train had been burned, a paymaster with sixty-three thousand dollars robbed, the passengers plundered of their hats, coats, boots, watches and money, and locking and burning the mail, express, and baggage, they made us a boisterous farewell.

The matter of my suggestion for a party to compete with Mosby, went through all the channels, up to Major General Halleck, the President's military adviser. I was informed that General Halleck approved of it, to give me a commission as Captain and Assistant Adjutant General, to report to the Adjutant General.

This was suggested to overcome rank restrictions. The matter, however, was delayed (I will refer to it again in March, 1865). The war ended without this scheme being accomplished. Meantime I declined to accept several tenders of commissions in promotion, expecting to realize this greater recognition.

The following tenders of promotion were declined:

Headquarters 8th N.Y. Arty.
before Petersburg, Va.,
Nov. 22, 1864.

Friend Smith.

How are you old boy and how have you enjoyed yourself since I last saw you? I am well, and full of fight as ever. We have done some fighting since we came into the field, and would like to have you with us.

There is a Captain's commission waiting for you if you will accept it. If you will send answer to me immediately, I will get it for you.

The officers of the Regiment would like to have you come. The Regiment is commanded by Major Baker, our Colonel (Willett) Commands the 1st Brigade, 2nd Div. 2nd Corps.

We have some good times and some d——d hard times, but I think it will pay.

I hope you will join us as Captain.

Good Bye,
J. W. Holmes,
Major 8th N.Y. H. Arty.
2nd Brig. 2nd Div. 2nd Corps.

Harper's Ferry, Va.
Dec. 15, 1864.

Dear Captain:

I suppose I have the right to address you by the above title now. Your Commission as Captain came yesterday and you will receive it by same mail as you do this.

Your Friend,   J. H. Graham.

Headquarters, Middle Department,
8th Army Corps.
Baltimore, Nov. 20, 1864.

Special Order No. 171.

Lieut. H. B. Smith, 5th N.Y. Arty. Comdg. Detective Corps 8th Army Corps, and one man as guard will at once proceed to Washington, D. C., in charge of prisoner J. J. Chancellor, on arrival at that point he will report with Chancellor, without delay, to Hon. C. A. Dana, Asst. Secretary of War. Having completed his duties at that place he will at once return with the guard to these headquarters.

Quartermasters will furnish necessary transportation.

By command of Major General Wallace.

Wm. H. Wiegel, Capt. & Asst. Provost Marshal.

Capture of Confederate Bonds and Scrip

I will now tell you of the Confederate bond matter. Special Order No. 172 enabled me to make my arrangements at Willard's Hotel:

> Headquarters, Middle Department,
> 8th Army Corps.
> Baltimore, Nov. 20, 1864.

Special Order No. 172.

Lieut. H. B. Smith, 5th N. Y., and one man will proceed to Washington, D. C., on secret service. On completion of his duties he will report with his guard at these headquarters.

By command of Major General Wallace.

> John Woolley,
> Lt. Col. & Pro. Marshal.

> Office Provost Marshal,
> Baltimore, Nov. 24, 1864.

Lt. Col. Woolley,

Provost Marshal.

Colonel.—I have the honour to report the arrest of J. S. Pittman, Dr. D. R. Brewer and T. S. Fowler.

I herewith hand you a carpet sack, containing Confederate Bonds and Scrip amounting to $82,575, which was collected in different ways from these parties. Also $22 from Dr. Brewer and $280 from Pittman, in currency, and a trunk said to contain 23 dozen cards (cotton and woollen cards) from Brewer's house.

Herewith I hand you several statements in reference to the case.

I would respectfully call your attention to Mr. Fowler's statement, *viz*.: that "that they sell this stuff to Jews, &c., that run the blockade," and that "it is all done for the benefit of the U. S. Service," and then to Pittman's statement that he did not know the New York man who was to buy of him in Washington, and then to my statement, *i. e.*, that I told him that I was from New York, and gave him my name and address in writing, and also told him how I intended to use the funds with blockade runners. Putting all these statements together I should conclude that if he is doing all this "for the benefit of the service," that he would have informed the authorities of my intentions.

Pittman's and Brewer's statements were made under oath. Brewer stated to me that the cards were bought to send to Dixie. In his sworn statement, after arrest, he declined giving the history of them, as it might injure his friends.

I am, Colonel,

Very respy. your obdt. servt.,

H. B. Smith,

Lt. & Chief.

This story is quite complicated. During the progress of this case, I was known to the parties as "Comings," "Shaffer" and Lieutenant Smith, and to show how complex it was, although Pittman and Brewer were together in prison, until trial came they had not been able to understand that the three names were for one person.

When I was about to go on the stand in their trial, their counsel asked me if Comings and Shaffer would be present? I answered yes; but when on the stand I began and told the story, their counsel claimed the Government had taken an advantage of them in concealing the facts.

Captain Hassing was my medium for getting into the case. It was a Baltimore gang, but either from suspicion of Hassing, or for other reasons, they would not meet the New York party (me) in Baltimore, so I arranged for a meeting in Washington, at Willard's Hotel. I went over and engaged a room there and registered; the following wire came:

Baltimore, Md.,

Nov. 20, 1864.

I. K. Shaffer,

Willards, Washington.

Have seen the parties arrangements are made for tomorrow be

here tonight.

Capt. Hassing.

In reply, I wired:

Washington, D. C.,
Nov. 20, 1864.

Capt. Hassing,
German St. Green House, Baltimore.
Telegram recd will meet you tomorrow evening at place appointed cannot close up my business with my friend here until morning.

I. K. Shaffer,
Willards Hotel.

The above telegram and the one following were for Hassing to exhibit to the gang, to show my earnestness:

Willards Hotel
Washington, Nov 21 1864

I. K. Shaffer
    Telegraph Office
        Barnum's Baltimore
Disposed of documents as you desired will see you in New York on 26. Your telegram recd.

G. B. Lyman.

I "fixed up" and went over to Washington on the same train with Pittman. I entered a forward car and Hassing saw to it that Pittman took one in the rear. At Washington I took a cab and landed in Willard's Hotel ahead of Pittman. Willard's, as you know, is in the shadow of the Treasury Department.

I was a sight to look upon; I wore a beaver, had my hair curled, had a birth mark on one cheek, and carried a cane; I was a New York swell in appearance surely. It almost made me sick to look in the mirror.

We introduced ourselves, each to the other, and then we went to my room. Pittman was very cautious; he said every other person in Washington was a detective. I assured him of my sympathy and told him that in New York we did not suffer from such surveillance. He said he was happy to become acquainted. He said he was so timid that he did not dare bring his bonds and scrip along, until after meeting me, when his confidence came to him, and said he would go over to Alexandria and return in the morning ready to do business.

We went down stairs; my two officers (Babcock and Horner), who

130

were following me to make the arrest when I indicated the propitious moment, were there. Pittman passed out the side entrance, and then Babcock and Horner invited him into their carriage. He protested, of course, but to no use; in the carriage they searched him and then hurried him on to Baltimore. They could not get out of him who had been with him up stairs in the hotel.

I then went into the barber shop, had my curls straightened, washed the birth mark off, and went to bed. In the morning I wired myself, using Pittman's name. The telegram I used as an introduction to Dr. Brewer, as follows:

Washington, D. C.,
Nov 22 1864

Geo. Comings
>   Washington Hotel
>   Baltimore

Go to see Dr. Brewer yourself. I will come on as soon as I see my mother in Alexandria. Telegraph me the result of your visit.

J. T. Pittman.

Dr. Brewer resided at the corner of Sharp and Conway Streets, not far from our office. I rang his bell and he responded. I unceremoniously rubbed my telegram under his nose as an introduction, giving him no chance to survey me. After considerable talk, explaining the necessity for my early return to New York, he said he would go and get the bonds and scrip. Having previously engaged a room at the Maltby House, I offered to walk with him, hoping thus to learn where the bonds were deposited, but that did not work. He later met me at the Maltby House, and we went up stairs to count over and settle; the two officers following to make the arrest when signalled, remained in the rotunda.

It took until dark came on to finish our business. We packed it all into a carpet sack. I gave Brewer $1,300 in currency, and then we went down stairs. The arrangement had been for my men to arrest him after he got far enough away from me, but so much time had elapsed, I presume my men had become careless, at any rate they were not in sight. I did not dare let Brewer get out of my reach, so I proposed to walk with him, to get some fresh air. When near his home, and when I had about made up my mind that I would have to make the arrest, to recover my $1,300, my men appeared; I skipped, and they made the arrest. Brewer was obstinate, but finally assumed a more reasonable attitude.

In their defence they tried to lighten the case by claiming the paper was forged, but when the Government demanded to know where they got the paper, they failed to inform.

Arrest of E. R. Rich, a Spy

Headquarters, Middle Department,
8th Army Corps.
Baltimore, Dec. 4, 1864.

Capt. W. H. Wiegel,

Asst. Provost Marshal.

Captain.—I have the honour to report that by direction of General Wallace, I arrested Mr. T. A. Menzier and locked him up in this jail, and ordered the officer of the Navy that was in company with him, Surgeon L. J. Draper, of the Receiving-Ship *Princeton*, Philadelphia Harbor, to report to you at ten o'clock a. m. today. These parties were in town yesterday morning and intend to return to Philadelphia this evening; neither of them had papers. Menzier's sister, at whose house I arrested them is a rebel.

The rebs were having a grand jubilee over his visit. The Doctor had no arms.

I am, Captain,

Very respy. your obdt. servt,

H. B. Smith,

Lt. & Chief.

I found in this house a number of prominent citizens, among whom was a very high officer in a big railroad company. He begged me not to report his presence, with which request I complied, in my written report, but did not, of course, fail to report verbally to General Wallace. This man was in confidential relations with the departments at Washington.

Menzier was a Rebel assistant surgeon. Both were turned over to

Commodore Dornin, for the Navy's disposition.

Headquarters, Middle Department,
8th Army Corps.
Baltimore, Dec. 5, 1864.

Capt. W. H. Wiegel,
Asst. Provost Marshal,
8th Army Corps.

Captain.—I have the honour to report that I confined Barton R. Zantzinger, from the Rebel Army.

Herewith I hand you his statement, which places Mr. Milnor Jones in a worse fix than ever. Perhaps this corroborative evidence will be sufficient to convict Jones of blockade running.

I think Zantzinger should be detained as a witness, if for nothing else.

I am Captain,
Very respy. your obdt. servt,
H. B. Smith,
Lt. & Chief.

Headquarters, Middle Department,
8th Army Corps.
Baltimore, Dec. 6, 1864.

Capt. W. H. Wiegel,
Asst. Provost Marshal,
8th Army Corps.

Captain.—I have the honour to report the arrest of John Henry Skinner Quinn, alias J. Y. Plater, alias Simpson, on charge of being a spy.

I hand you two sworn statements that he made to me, also his memorandum book in which is a partial description of his first visit to Baltimore, also some entries, some of which he explains in his statement. I also hand you his furlough, which he said he did not have, in his first statement.

On this trip he registered at Miller's Hotel as "Simpson." On 23rd April last, he registered at same hotel as John Y. Plater.

You can see by his statements that he tries to conceal the Rebel sympathizers of this Department, and some he positively refuses to name, but asks me to kill him, and not ask him any more questions.

He came to this office to report as a Rebel deserter, but when he found that I had been on his track, he owned up, but refused to implicate his friends.

I am, Captain,

Very respy. your obdt. servt.,

H. B. Smith,

Lt. & Chief.

As General Wallace had said, it was our duty to ascertain by every means, the status of all persons; our archives were crowded with information, which materially helped us to avoid the dilemma General Schenck described.

Headquarters, Middle Department,

8th Army Corps.

Baltimore, Dec. 7, 1864.

Capt. W. H. Wiegel,

Asst. Provost Marshal,

8th Army Corps.

Captain.—I have the honour to report the arrest of E. R. Rich, of the 1st Md. Rebel Cavalry, on the charge of being a spy. He came to this office to report and take the oath of allegiance, but I think he did not come until he heard from his friend Quinn, with whom he came to this city. I hand you herewith his sworn statement, memoranda and pocket book, which show his character.

You will also see an entry in his memoranda where Skinner Quinn (now in prison) started for Baltimore last spring, which corroborates Quinn's statement. You will also see that he registered under several names.

The memorandum book shows that it was his intention to return for good to Virginia.

Very respy. your obdt. servt,

H. B. Smith,

Lt. & Chief.

Both Quinn and Rich were sentenced to be hanged, but their sentences were finally commuted to imprisonment during the continuance of the war.

Report on Daniel W. Jones and Joseph Bratton

Headquarters, Middle Department,
8th Army Corps.
Baltimore, Dec. 10, 1864.

Lt. Col. Woolley,

Provost Marshal.

Colonel.—I have the honour to hand you statement made by Illinois Crothers, of 1st Md. Rebel Cavalry, who came to this office to report.

I questioned him closely and on every point of importance, he seemed very ignorant. He was in this city several days without reporting, and to all appearances is as bitter a Rebel today as ever.

I took from him a document marked "A," which shows that it was generally known to the authorities in Virginia, that he was coming to Maryland, and unless they were sure he would return, he would not have been granted the liberty. You can also see that he came an unusual route, for a deserter, i. e., by the way of Richmond.

I have reliable information that all of the Rebel Spies, commissioned as such, are from the Signal Corps.

Harry Brogden, named in the document, was once in our hands, tried as a spy. Herewith I hand you Brogden's history.

I think that this document shows that he, (Crothers), came with the consent of the Rebel authorities, and with the intention to return.

I am, Colonel,

Very respy. your obdt. servt.,

H. B. Smith,

Lt. & Chief.

P.S.—Mrs. Keenan, of Winchester, should be arrested.
This is not the first transaction of the kind implicating Mr. Wm. Mitchell. (H. B. S.)

It required experience and skill to cull out the spies from among real deserters and refugees. Spies would swallow the oath of allegiance as easy as water. One of the best tests of probabilities, was to ascertain the route travelled in coming out from the Confederacy.

Harry Brogden was the Confederate secret signal officer on the Potomac. No real deserter or refugee came by his way. I knew him, and if my operations had been extended to the peninsula between the Potomac and Rappahannock, as we desired, I would have caught him; personally he was a fine fellow. He was a prisoner at Fort McHenry under me; he and I joked about turning our "arms into ploughshares" many times. He was certainly as loyal to his side as I to mine.

The following is a report made from the records in my office, and it serves to show how thorough in detail our data had come to be:

Headquarters, Middle Department,

8th Army Corps. Baltimore,

Dec. 13, 1864.

Lt. Col. John Woolley,

Provost Marshal,

8th Army Corps.

Colonel.—I have the honour to give you a history of the previous arrests of Daniel W. Jones, and Joseph Bratton, of Somerset Co., Md.

The first arrest of Daniel W. Jones was made in 1862, and he was placed in Marshal McPhail's custody, under charge of attacking an enrolling officer. He was afterwards released on giving bonds to the amount of $2,000 to keep the peace, and to deport himself in every way becoming a loyal citizen. A copy of the bond is on file in this office.

He was again arrested by General Lockwood, May 7, 1864, on charge of having violated his parole; on this last charge four sworn statements are on file in this office, one to the effect that he drew a revolver on a Union man because said Union man declared his sentiments.

Joseph Bratton was arrested March 31, 1864, on the charge of disloyalty, and aiding the Rebels. A sworn statement now on file in this office shows that Bratton aided an escaped prisoner from Point Lookout to evade military and get back within the Rebel lines.

I am, Colonel,

Very respy. your obdt. servt.,

H. B. Smith,

Lt. & Chief.

The following gave me unlimited access to our prisoners confined in the city jail:

Headquarters, Middle Department,

8th Army Corps.

Baltimore, Dec. 19, 1864.

Col. Thomas C. James,

Warden, City Jail.

The bearer, Lieut. H. B. Smith, 5th N. Y. H. Arty., who commands my detective Corps, is permitted to see any prisoner in the City Jail who belongs to this office, and at such times as he may deem necessary for the good of the service.

He will be permitted to have private interviews if he desires them.

By command of Major General Wallace.

John Woolley,

Lt. Col. & Pro. Marshal.

Charles E. Langley, an Official Confederate Spy

I have told you that it required experience and skill to determine who were honest deserters, sick of the Confederate service, and seeking homes in our lines, or who were refugees, entitled to a refuge, or who were spies. Under the head of spies were placed those who came North to visit friends, or gain a remount intending to return to the Confederate lines; these latter were not being especially employed as spies, but they were persons who might carry valuable information. But it was the real official spy that we were after.

By a "remount" I mean those who were granted leave of absence by the Confederates for the purpose of remounting. These were mounted men who having lost their horses, were given a "remount pass" which was practically authority to come within our lines and gain a horse by any means; therefore without desire to weary you I will give you the examinations of one of each class, to wit: Jeremiah Artis, a real deserter; Wm. J. Bradley, a refugee; Charles E. Langley, one of the most expert and successful official spies, who is the one I referred to in the Emmerich case as the "pal" of the conductor on the Baltimore and Ohio railroad.

In reading these statements, you will notice jumps, or gaps, where these occur; it indicates a question from me eliciting the statement following.

Statement of Jeremiah Artis (real deserter).

I kept store in Smithville, St. Mary's County, seven or eight miles from Point Lookout, about one and a half miles from the Bay. I joined the 1st Va. Cav., then was transferred to the 1st

Md. Cav., was then transferred to the 2nd Md. Infty., Com'd by Capt. Crane. Lt. Col. Herbert is the field officer. I left Md. Sep. 1861, crossed the Potomac at night. I first heard of the President's proclamation, saw it in a Baltimore paper sometime early in the spring of 1864, the paper was an old one. I was in Maryland at the battle of Antietam or Sharpsburg, was also at Gettysburg, was transferred from Cavalry to Infantry but wouldn't stay, rejoined the Cavalry, was with Bradley T. Johnson at Chambersburg; had no hand in burning it, was kept outside of the city. I had been arrested while trying to cross the Potomac in July, was kept in Richmond awhile, then sent to my Regiment. Got as far as Winchester when Early came into Maryland. When I was arrested, I was trying to get home to stay; was on the Virginia side at the time I was arrested by the conscription officers. When I was in Maryland I would have deserted but had no chance.

I left my Regiment this last time about Sept. 22 or 23rd, in the Shenandoah Valley, near Port Republic, crossed Brown's Gap, then through Green County, Madison, Orange, Spottsylvania, Stafford, King George, Westmorland Counties, to Northumberland County to the Potomac River, crossed over to Britton's Bay. I had no furlough or pass. The Confederate Army was moving at the time and I had no trouble in going through the country.

If I had been arrested I would have said I belonged to no regiment, as my time was out. I walked from Britton's Bay direct to the Patuxent River to Spencer's Wharf, and took steamboat to Baltimore, arrived there at 11 at night and slept at a hotel; next morning I reported to the Provost Marshal's office. I had no uniform except a jacket that I threw away in Virginia, near the river. I bought a coat from some young men I saw there.

D. Hammell came with me all the time. I expected when I reported to be allowed to take the oath of allegiance and to be allowed to remain at home. I prefer soldiering to anything else in the world, and if I was as strong a Southern man as I was when I first went away, I would stay in the Rebel army, no matter how much hardship I would have to endure. I think I could be a truly loyal citizen.

When I landed at Britton's Bay I did not go home because I wished to come to Baltimore and report. I knew there was a

Provost Marshal to report to in Baltimore. Have seen no new recruits from Maryland in our regiment lately. We got a few recruits while in Maryland this last time. I did not know any of them, or where they were from; there were very few. I don't think our Company got any of them. Captain Brown was formerly our Captain; he was killed.

STATEMENT OF WILLIAM J. BRADLEY
(A REFUGEE), A CALIFORNIAN:

(*Dec. 31, 1864.*) I left Richmond, Virginia, on Dec. 11th. I was given the following directions and a pass by order of the Rebel Secretary of War, to come North; the directions were given by the Chief Signal Officer, *viz*: get off the cars at Milford, see Boles at Bowling Green, Gibbs at Port Royal, Rollins at Port Conway. I went to Oak Grove one and a half miles from the Signal Camp. The Signal Camp is on Bridge Creek, five miles from its mouth. At a point on the creek where there was an old bridge which was burned, is where you strike the road that leads to camp, which camp is about three hundred yards from the creek, and on the site of the birth place of Washington. They have a boat there in which they cross the Potomac; it is about twenty-six feet long, and capable of carrying about sixteen persons; they keep it about three-quarters of a mile above, on the creek.

At the Signal Camp I saw about twelve men, commanded by Sergeant Harry Brogden; they were armed with revolvers. They collect passes that are granted in Richmond, run the mail and Rebel agents North, and back again. They told me they were expecting some twelve or fifteen parties back from Maryland again, very soon.

When I came over in the boat it was manned by four oarsmen and one steersman, and as passengers, Norris, an Englishman and myself, and brought over a mail. We landed at Cobb Neck. Morris said he would start back from the other side of the Wicomico.

The following are additional names of members of the Signal Corps:

    —— Rowley.
    —— Reed, formerly a boatman on the Potomac.
    —— Brockenborough.

These men said they were daily expecting members of Mosby's command on the Neck.

The route Bradley came was the exact route of the regular spies; but the information he gave me was of a character to prove that although he came by the official route, he was being honest with me. Some of the information was new, and all of it was true and valuable. I drew out the detailed information about the signal camp to guide me. I was determined to capture it, and in April following my expedition was planned to start, but was prevented by the assassination of the President.

Baltimore City Jail,
Dec. 23, 1864.

STATEMENT OF CHARLES E. LANGLEY

(OFFICIAL CONFEDERATE SPY).

I was born and raised in Winchester, Virginia. I resided in Baltimore some time previous to the breaking out of the war. I was in Washington at the Inauguration of President Lincoln; was keeping a butter store in Baltimore.

In the summer of 1861, or perhaps early in the fall, I went to Winchester; my parents resided there. The cars ran through to Winchester. I went on the cars, no passes were required from me on the road. The Confederate troops occupied Winchester at the time. I went to work on the Winchester Railroad after I arrived; worked a short time. I remained at Winchester all that winter; was not in the army.

The next spring (1862), I went to Richmond. Went to work driving an express wagon. Worked at that until the next fall. I worked for the Southern Express Co.; a man named Holbrook, from Baltimore, was at work for the Express Co. at the same time. The draft came off that fall and I left for Winchester to escape it. I tried to pretend I was from Maryland, and therefore exempt, but as I was too well known it would not work. I did nothing after I returned to Winchester, and staid there till Christmas. The town was then occupied by Union troops. About the last of Jan. 1863, I visited Baltimore and tried to get a situation; I remained in Baltimore about two months, doing nothing. I stopped at Mann's Hotel, that is, I got my meals there, as I wanted them. I stopped part of the time with "Bonis," a tinner, out Fayette street; I used to board with them before the war.

I went back to Winchester about the first of March, but could get nothing to do. I staid about a couple of weeks and then came back to Baltimore. I tried again to get work here, tried to get on the Baltimore & Ohio Railroad. I worked on that road before the war, about three or four years. I offered my services to Mr. Smith, Master of Transportation, as a kind of scout for them, to ascertain when the road was injured, and where, and other information relative to the safety of the road. I did go up the road for him on several occasions in 1863 and gave him satisfaction.

I went up the road for Mr. Smith at the time Lee was crossing into Maryland; could not get back, and went home to Winchester; the Rebels occupied the town. I was arrested for being in Maryland, as a Yankee spy, was kept about a week and then discharged, as they had no proof and my friends in Winchester got me off.

In the fall of 1863, when the Rebels left, I came back to Baltimore. I went to see Mr. Smith, but could not get any work from him. I remained in Baltimore until about Nov. 1st, when I went on to New York to make arrangements with Mr. Sydney H. Gay, to obtain Richmond papers for him. Mr. Gay is connected with the *Tribune*; I went to work for him, used to go down the valley to Winchester and obtain papers from parties down the valley, further south than Winchester. I was successful in obtaining papers but could have done better if I had had an assistant. I don't think I gave my employer justice, but I remained there to do the best I could. I continued in this business until April 1st, 1864. I was stopped part of the time on account of want of means; my pay was not sufficient to enable me to make proper arrangements.

I remained in Winchester about two weeks trying to make arrangements. I would not tell who I obtained the papers from in the valley. I used to bring the papers as far as Kearneysville. I always reported to the Provost Marshal at Kearneysville when I arrived there, of any information I had obtained of the (Rebel) enemy.

I went down the valley to a friend, near Strausburg, to see about getting the papers more regularly. I got inside the Rebel lines and could not get out. I remained inside their lines at New

Market, with some friends, about six weeks. I staid there until the fight with Sigel. That very day Breckenridge had me arrested for holding communication with the Federal troops. I was kept in confinement two months, and afterwards in arrest under three thousand dollars bail for five months.

About Sept. 1st, I came up to Winchester to my home, and was ordered back again. I went back and staid until about October, the last of the month. I then crossed the Ridge and made my way to Harper's Ferry. I got on the cars at Van Kleeve's Station, Baltimore & Ohio Railroad, and came on to Baltimore. I arrived here about the last of October. I stopped at Mr. Perigoy's, No. 34 George street; his wife is a distant relative of mine. I was not doing anything in particular, intended to go to New York to see Mr. Gay. I was also trying to find out who caused me to be arrested by Breckenridge, as I was confident some Rebels in Baltimore were the cause of it.

I also heard that Breckenridge said a citizen of Kearneysville had reported me as having given information to the A. Adjutant General at Harper's Ferry.

I was arrested Sunday night on the street on my way home, by Government detectives. I gave them a false name. I never was in the Rebel army. Have never taken the oath of allegiance; have never been asked to take it; think my arrest was not justified.

(Signed)   Chas. E. Langley.

I followed this man a year. After I arrested him very powerful interests tried to frighten me; tried to make me believe the prisoner was such an important person that his name must be whispered only. That, in fact, he was Mr. Lincoln's personal man, and reporting only to Mr. Lincoln. They threatened to have my commission taken from me. Finally the prisoner himself offered to give up the "hotel burners" of New York, if I would let up. I answered that I thought "a bird in hand worth two in the bush," and I held him.

Upon his person I found his authority from the New York *Tribune* to collect news at the front. This authority had been his open sesame through our lines. I came to New York and saw Mr. Sidney B. Gay, of the *Tribune*; he informed me that he remembered such a person, that he came to him highly recommended; that he gave him the authority but had never heard from him. I learned later that the powerful interests that were working on me to compel his release were the same that

CHARLES E. LANGLEY

had highly recommended him to the *Tribune*. He was a very successful and dangerous spy until I interfered.

I will not tell you who the powerful interests were; suffice it to say they were Confederates, doing good work for the Confederacy all the while. Yet they had the entree of the departments at Washington, having very powerful influence there. There were no other parties in the United States so strongly allied. Through their medium many strange things were manipulated. I will not mention their names, for they are all dead now. I consider Langley's arrest one of the most important.

Of all the newspapers the *Tribune* was the very best to conjure with. Any person who could show credentials from that paper would undoubtedly be welcome anywhere on our lines.

Langley knew that I would visit the *Tribune*, hence his efforts in his statement to account for why he had not served them.

FILE 29

A Sketch of the Defences
of Richmond

The following statement is interesting as showing how a poor, ignorant, drunken man was hurried off with Gilmor and Bradley T. Johnson, in July, '64, when they retreated from north of Baltimore.

I feel sure the whiskey was paid for by Judge Grason, or Mr. Cockey, or some of the other disloyals spoken of in Mr. Kremer's and my own former reports. They undoubtedly gave him the horse, also:

Baltimore, Md.,
Dec. 23, 1864.

STATEMENT OF PATRICK SCALLY

I was born in Ireland. I lived in Texas, Baltimore County, for five years before I went South; my father and mother live there. I am a laborer.

I went South on the tenth of last July, that is, I joined Gilmor's command at Texas. I joined Company C, Second Maryland Battalion. They gave me a horse, carbine and sabre. The second day after I joined them I was in the fight in front of Washington, but did not like the fighting much.

I was drunk when I joined them and didn't know what I was doing.

I deserted from them on the 1st day of August between Hancock and Cumberland, and went to work for a farmer named McLean, a good Union man; he didn't know that I was a deserter. I worked for him about two weeks. I then went to Cumberland, and then went to Pittsburg and there worked for Wood, Matthews & Co., nearly four months. I was afraid, while at work for Mr. McLean, that the Rebels would catch me and shoot me.

I didn't report at Pittsburg because I didn't know there was any necessity for so doing; the people in Pittsburg did not know that I had been with the Rebels. I was only with the Rebels three weeks, they never gave me a uniform; they once paid me ten dollars in Confederate money.

I was sworn into the Rebel service the same day that I enlisted, while I was drunk. I wore the same citizens clothes that I wore from home, while with the Rebels. I would have deserted the next morning after I joined them if I could, but could not get any chance.

I left Pittsburg last Sunday night, got home to Texas yesterday evening. My father told me I would have to come here and take the oath and if I did not I would be arrested as a spy. I knew I had to give myself up before. I came in town this morning and gave myself up.

I cannot read or write. I have heard the newspapers read, but not often. I never heard of the President's Proclamation, don't know what it is."

his

(Signed)   Patrick X Scally.

mark

Below is a sketch of the fortifications bounding Richmond on the east and north. The information came to me from Dr. A's brother, who had just arrived from Richmond. The source of information being so reliable, a copy was made and forwarded to General Grant. The date of its transmission I have not.

When General Grant made the assault on Richmond, on the east and north, on Sept. 26, 1864, the coloured troops under General Birney encountered this ditch.

I quote from reports:

On Sep. 28th a movement was made by General Grant on the North of the James. It was predicated on the belief that only a small force of the enemy occupied the works on the North side of the river.

General Birney was ordered by a rapid movement at daylight, to capture the enemy's work in front of Deep Bottom, and gain

Defences of Richmond on North and East. Information from Dr B Bodther Asst Engd U.S. Grant for this information

Trench — 15 Wide — 11 deep
Rifle pits

Richmond Pike

ditch 15 by 11 feet

11 inch Columbiads

possession of the New Market road leading to Richmond.

Two Regiments only, of the Coloured Division, reached one of the Rebel forts, where they found a ditch ten feet wide and eight feet deep between them and the parapet.

More than a hundred of these brave fellows jumped into the ditch and assisted some of their comrades to mount the parapet by allowing them to climb up on their shoulders, about a dozen succeeded in mounting the parapet by this means. But this force which had bravely pushed on, was far too small to capture the fort, and was, therefore, compelled to retire, leaving their comrades in the ditch of the fort.

But these were unable to make good their escape, as it would have been certain death to leave the ditch and return to the troops, and were afterwards compelled to surrender.

About 800 men were lost in this assault in killed, wounded, and prisoners.

I regret not having the date upon which my information was forwarded to General Grant, but it evidently was not in his hand by September 28th.

COLONEL HARRY GILMOR

The Arrest and Conviction of
the Fair Donor

Colonel Harry Gilmor, who commanded a regiment of cavalry in the Confederate service, was a Baltimorean. He was the beau ideal of its "blue blood" ladies, or many of them; he was their hero who was to ultimately capture the Monumental City, who was to march down Charles Street Avenue as conquerors only return. He had earnestly tried to produce the closing scene of his drama in July, but failed; when, to cheer him to renew his efforts, they proposed to present him with a magnificent sabre. They purchased the best to be found from Messrs. Schuyler, Hartley & Graham, arms dealers, then in Maiden Lane, New York (now on Broadway), paying for it one hundred and twenty-five dollars in gold.

I was told the dainty creatures were so anxious for the safe custody of their token of war, that they placed it under the British flag, pending the opportunity to get it to the Colonel; that is, they left it with Mrs. Frederick Bernal, wife of the British Consul at Baltimore. The sympathies of many of the Britishers were decidedly with the South.

Gilmor was a born raider. He used to raid the hearts of these Blue Belles "befo de wah," on Charles Street Avenue. His command was made up largely of Marylanders, and Maryland was frequently the victim of his incursions. Our desire to "possess" him was perhaps as great as that of any of his lady admirers.

On November 1st, 1864, I intercepted the sword on its way to Harry. From the person of the messenger I got a letter which was to make him "solid" when he should arrive in the Confederate territory. Gilmor was understood to have been wounded, and as being then laid up at the Inglenby Mansion, three or four miles from Duffield Station,

Virginia, on the Baltimore and Ohio Railroad (the Inglenby family were descendants of one of the original colonists).

The letter was somewhat blindly framed, it did not mention the bearer, except to say that "he is perfectly reliable" or something to that effect.

I proposed to General Wallace that I would be the messenger, using this letter, and would thus locate Gilmor, so that he might be captured.

With one man, Mr. Kraft, I started for Harper's Ferry, reported to General Stevenson, engaged one of his scouts, Corporal George R. Redman (who at one time was of my corps) to go with me and equipped with the below described pass, I started out on the Baltimore and Ohio Railroad for Duffield Station.

Office Provost Marshal,
Military District of Harper's Ferry.
Nov. 5, 1864.

Guards and Pickets will pass bearer in and around this Military District. Good for three days.

By order of

Brigadier General Stevenson,
Commanding.

A. D. Pratt,
Capt. & Provost Marshal.

It was my custom never to have about me anything to indicate my name or identity. And to conceal my passes, I frequently hammered them down into a small wad in the finger of a glove. This pass shows such an appearance. The pass did not indicate Duffield, because that destination was a secret.

Duffield was a small way station, and any stranger alighting there, especially in those days, would be noted. Many of the employees of the Baltimore and Ohio Railroad were Confederate sympathizers (some were quite active). To give no chance for warning, we waited until just after the train started up, and then we dropped off, on the far side, covering view of us until the train was again under headway.

We separated and I went ahead, across fields, until I was so far away as to apparently have no connection with my men, who were following; we had about three or four miles to go thus. Finally, when I reached the Inglenby house, my boys were near enough to be in sight, yet concealed.

At the house I introduced myself and presented my letter. For the purpose, I represented myself as a Baltimorean, of course—a "hack driver at Barnum's Hotel," I learned that Gilmor had been there, but only recently had gone down the valley. I told them of the sword, that the donors wanted to learn how to reach Colonel Gilmor, accurately; hence my trip. They treated me very nicely, prepared a good meal for me with true Virginia hospitality; finally I departed.

When I arrived where the boys were concealed, I found them extremely anxious to get away from that section. While they were laying there a man had approached them, saying that he knew they were "deserters from the Yanks"; the boys admitted it. He asked them if they wanted to go South. They told him "yes." He told them he knew it, and after it got dark he would take them. He told them that some of Mosby's men were just over on the road. My boys were not really hungry to go South, but wanted to start across the country for Harper's Ferry without delay, which we did, arriving there late in the evening, in the custody of our own pickets, who had captured us at Halltown.

Had I reached Gilmor I believe I might have tried to capture him, had I found the odds favourable. He was a giant in stature. How game he was I do not know. I will give you a reproduction of his photograph, which I have.

Upon my return to Baltimore I arrested the representative fair donor of the sabre, as General Wallace has told. She resided in the ultra fashionable neighbourhood, not far from Monument Square. After I had searched her house, she accompanied me to the sidewalk, but absolutely refused to enter my carriage. I informed her that it would be much more agreeable to ride than to walk, but still she refused. I then told her that I would be gentlemanly if allowed, but I insisted that she must get into the carriage. She finally complied.

The lady was tried before a military commission of which Lieutenant Colonel J. H. Barrett was president. She was sentenced to five years imprisonment at Fitchburg, Massachusetts, and to pay a fine of five thousand dollars.

A Mr. William J. Ives, who purchased the sword in New York, was also tried. He escaped punishment on the plea that he was ignorant of the purpose for which the sword was purchased.

One of Gilmor's officers I subsequently captured. He had come into our lines, having one of those "remount" leaves from his command. It was not proposed to treat him as severely as a spy, but to hold him as a prisoner of war. I did not make him aware of this, however, but left him under the stress of the impression that he might fear the worst, and I proposed to him that we would permit him to return to his command provided he would agree to make it easy for General Sheridan's scouts to capture Harry. I knew my man and had confidence he would carry out his part of the bargain, especially since the stake played for was, as he supposed, his life. I let him go, and advised General Sheridan of the arrangement. The following is the acknowledgment of my communication:

Provost Marshal's office,
Headquarters, Middle Military Division.
Winchester, Va., Jany. 25, 1865.
Lieut. Smith.

Dear Sir.—I have submitted your communication to General Sheridan, and he has taken action in the case.

With respect,
John A. Gernos.

The expedition connected with the following pass through the pickets at Harper's Ferry was pertaining to Gilmor's capture:

Office Provost Marshal,
Military District of Harper's Ferry.
Jany. 27, 1865.

Guards and Pickets will pass Capt. H. B. Smith to any place about the Ferry, Sandy Hook, or Berlin.

Good for two days.

By order of Brigadier General Stevenson.
A. D. Pratt,
Major & Provost Marshal.

On February 6th, 1865, Gilmor was captured by General Sheridan. Major Young, Chief of his Scouts, brought him to Colonel Woolley's office, on his way to prison in Fort Warren. Mr. W. G. Woodside, paymaster of the Baltimore and Ohio Railroad, a mutual (?) friend of Gilmor and myself, came to my office and invited me to be introduced, saying that Harry said he knew me. General Woolley's office was crowded. Gilmor was asked by Mr. Woodside to point me out, but he could not. I had never advertised my face very much; it better suited my purposes to be unknown.

Gilmor said to me, if he had had the sword, he would have killed many a Yank with it. A safe enough proposition under the circumstances. Gilmor in appearance was attractive, as a soldier, tall, fairly stout, but he had one defective eye and was rather coarse in manners.

After the war I saw the officer of Gilmor's regiment who had been our prisoner and who agreed to surrender Gilmor, or rather make his capture possible. I was sorry to see that he had become dissipated. He told me the cause was his social ostracism by the "Blue Bloods." I have never mentioned his name, and never will. I have, I think a fair amount of moral tone, and I cannot see that this man's act was low. He supposed that he was obtaining the privilege to live, in exchange for the mere incarceration of Gilmor. It was not the trading of a life for a life. I sincerely trust the young man has not suffered a lifetime for the act.

On June 15th, 1873, I received from Gilmor the following letter:

Baltimore, Md.,
15th June, 1873.

Lt. H. B. Smith,
    New York.

My Dear Sir.—I have been trying for some time past to learn your address, and hope I have at last succeeded, with the assistance of Major Wiegel.

My object in writing is to know whether or not you still have in your possession the sword which the ladies of Baltimore intended for me, but which fell into your hands.

If you have the sword still, and would be willing to dispose of it, will you say what you will take for it, as I would like very much to own it, if it did not cost too much.

I have been lately elected to the Command of a Battalion of Cavalry in this city, composed of men who were on both sides during the "late unpleasantness," and am very anxious to make a fine battalion of it.

If you will do me the favour to communicate with me on this subject I will be very grateful.

    Address, very truly yours,

Harry Gilmor,
Cor. President & Fawn Streets,
Baltimore, Md.

At that time everything was being done to "heal the wound" and I was disposed to do my little part. I was disposed to present the sword to him, first getting General Wallace's approval. But on conferring with Union people of Baltimore, I concluded not to; they thought any ostentatious display of the sword would help keep the wound open.

Steam tug *Grace Titus*

Depot Quartermaster's Office,
Baltimore, Jany. 16, 1865.

Captain, Steam Tug
   Grace Titus.

You will proceed with your tug as directed by Lieut. H. B. Smith, who will hand you this.

Upon completion of the service demanded by Lieut. Smith, you will return to this port and report to me.

Respectfully,

A. M. Cummings,

Capt. & Quartermaster.

I cannot recall what the expedition was for. Incidentally, I may say, I am continually recognizing that many good stories will be omitted from lapses of memory, but you will not lose much, as the ones I am furnishing serve to show the general varied character of my work. My own personal work and the work of my men, employed in every direction, kept me busy. I had a man on every steamer plying Chesapeake Bay.

In glancing over subpoenas to attend courts, I find name after name, none of which occur here; but the most important proposition before me was to gather information that would assist me in my proposed work to cripple Mosby's damaging work in the territory known as "between the lines." It was the country outside our lines and outside the Confederate lines, peopled by our enemies, always willing to serve the Confederacy, never serving us; acting as a sponge to draw supplies from us by means of blockade-running, which could in turn be absorbed by the Confederates. The efforts of our gunboats to stop the traffic were futile, as I have heretofore remarked.

Office Provost Marshal,
8th Army Corps.
Baltimore, Jany. 19, 1865.

STATEMENT OF GEORGE CARLTON, DESERTER,

BATTERY BALTIMORE, REBEL HORSE ARTILLERY, SAYS:

I am a native of Brooklyn, New York. Went South in the year 1859; went to Mobile. I was engaged in a dry goods store. In May, 1862, I was put in the Rebel Army at Richmond, which place I was taken to from Mobile. I had the chance to join what command I pleased and I joined the Baltimore Battery in Richmond. I staid in the company two weeks, then was detailed in the Quartermaster's Department at Gordonsville, Va.

I remained there until the spring of 1864, when I was sent to my Company, then in the valley, under Early. I staid with the Company until Oct. 1864, when I deserted from my Company and came to Westmorland County, Va., and then took a boat and crossed the Potomac River and landed in St. Mary's County, Md., and from there I walked to Baltimore.

I was afraid to attempt to desert before that time. (Oct. '64.) I deserted during Early's retreat. The Battery that I was a member of lost all their guns. I heard officers say that they lost forty-four pieces.

I had a hard time getting through Westmorland County. I did not cross the river until about two weeks ago, and during that time I have been on my way from St. Mary's County to this city.

Now I wish to give certain information to the Government: John J. Spaulding, who lived near Leonardtown, Md., and now lives on the Virginia side, at Westmorland Court House, six miles from the Potomac River, and boarding with a Mr Harvey, who keeps tavern at the Court House, brought me over the river and eight persons besides myself.

He brought us over in the night; he seemed very much afraid, and kept out of sight, and landed at Caywood's Bluff, near Britton's Bay.

Spaulding is a blockade runner, and keeps a large store of blockade goods at Westmorland Court House. He brought a large lot over the river a few days before I arrived at the Court House.

He keeps his boat in Poor Jack Creek, and in a small gut. From what I heard, I think when he comes over after goods he goes to St. Clemmen's Bay in St. Mary's County, up to a certain Merryman's store, and I know that Merryman sells goods to Spaulding and a much larger quantity to Watkins & Pumphrey, two blockade runners at the Court House.

Pumphrey did belong to my company; Watkins to the 1st Maryland Infantry (Rebel) and deserted, and they are now running the blockade.

Watkins and Pumphrey were over about a month ago, and while on their way up St. Clemmen's Bay, while landing in a creek near Merryman's store, the Federal Cavalry, being informed by a citizen came near capturing them, but they hid in their hiding place, and then they went in the night to Merryman's store; he told them that if they were not more careful, he would not sell them goods.

Pumphrey told me about it when he came back to the Court House. They bought at that time about five hundred dollars' worth of goods; Pumphrey showed me the bill made out by Merryman. The kind and quantity of goods were, sugar, coffee, dry-goods, gray cloth, hats, boots and shoes, gun-caps, powder spices and other goods, shot, &c.

"I have seen them haul the goods from the boat to the Court House, and have seen most of the things, including the powder and caps on Merryman's bill. The powder came over in cans, weighing about five pounds each. The party who hauls the stuff from Merryman's store to the boat is named Bows, or Bowers, who lives near Leonardtown.

Jarboe and Molacy, blockade runners who were captured, bought their goods of Merryman, sometimes. Certain vessels running wood from near Leonardtown to Washington or Alexandria as a pretext, drop in on the Virginia shore and land goods and recruits for the Rebel Army, so I learned at the Court House.

John J. Spaulding had a brother, a Doctor, in Leonardtown, who forwarded goods to the river shore for his brother John; he, Dr Spaulding, was drafted and ordered to report. He deserted and went over to the Virginia shore to his brother, and took Blair, Bailey Bowers, a son of the man who hauls goods, and Hayden; they were all drafted men.

Since Dr. Spaulding left this side, his wife, Mrs. Dr. Eck Spaulding, has attended to all the business in that line; she has the name on the Virginia side of being the smartest of the three in that business. The Spauldings told me that she forwarded stuff to them.

They understood that I had a furlough and that I was on my way to Maryland to make what I could and return to Virginia. John Harvey, the keeper of the tavern, runs refugees over the river, but I can't say whether he brings goods back or not, but runners say he does.

While I was at Westmorland Court House, some four companies out of seven, of Mosby's men, came down and camped at Heathesville, some twenty or twenty-five miles from where I was. They intended to winter their horses there. Mosby was not in command; they were commanded by a Major. I heard Mosby was wounded.

John J. Spaulding showed me a bill of exchange, fifteen pounds sterling, on Brown Brothers and Company, Baltimore, in favour of Thomas Levering. John J. Spaulding, on arrival on this side, passed it into the hands of Dr. Spaulding's wife, for collection.

About six weeks ago Spaulding brought over to the Md. shore, a Lieut. Smith, of Mosby's command, and Russel Low, and Daniel DeWolf Low, and at another time Wm. H. Sweeney, of Washington; he is engaged to get married, and came over to get wedding clothes. Sweeney has been over before, in company with Watkins.

Spaulding also brought over a man by the name of Richy, who was a detective in Richmond, and has carried two Rebel mails to Richmond from Maryland. Spaulding also brought over one Carroll, of Baltimore; also some Jew blockade runners, and a great many others. The Jews run a great deal of medicine for the Confederate Government.

It is my opinion that a cavalry force, landed above on the Neck, could cut Mosby's four companies off, and capture them in the position they lay.

There is a Signal Post on the Potomac River, near Mathias Point, Va., in charge of Captain Caywood, of the Confederate Signal Corps. He has a boat, and in good weather he comes over twice a week. He carries the regular mail and the foreign mail; it is a regular government concern.

I tried to find out who assisted him on this side, but could not do so. I found he would carry no one over without a pass from the Secretary of War. In crossing the river they sometime pass within 1200 yards of a gunboat.

(Signed and sworn.)

"Boney" Lee, Bob Miller, and Other Thugs

Office of Provost Marshal General
for Maryland.
Baltimore, Jany. 19, 1865.

Capt. Smith,
Asst. Provost Marshal.

Sir.—The pungy *Trifle* now stands in the name of Conrad Prince. She changed owners on the 10th of June, last.

She had not cleared by permit since then, but may have done so by manifest.

Yours, &c.,

McPhail.

Colonel McPhail was the Civil Provost Marshal of Maryland, having exclusively to do with enrolments and drafts; the office was entirely separated from the military service. He was a very clean, upright, honourable man. There was, however, a district under him, having at its head a Major Blumenburg, that was very corrupt.

Soldiers were fleeced out of bounty money. Substitutes, quite frequently colored men, were paid large sums as bounties, more money than they had ever seen before. By collusion between officers and clerks in Blumenburg's office, and the substitute brokers, the substitutes were induced to invest in valueless gewgaws, sometimes paying for a two-dollar Oride watch as much as one hundred dollars.

One of the largest substitute brokerage concerns tried to reach me with an offer of five hundred dollars a week, for a period as long as I would let them alone. The offer was not "dangerously near my price." I cleaned up the whole business very soon.

Blumenburg appointed a lot of cut throats with authority to arrest deserters, paying them ten dollars for each deserter brought in. Their operations were conducted this way: One of these fellows would hail a soldier who was out on pass take it away from him, pronouncing it fraudulent, but would allow him to proceed on his way; shortly he would be hailed again, by a "pal," and having, of course, no pass to exhibit, he would be arrested charged with desertion.

I was over in Anne Arundel County one night with three or four of my men, intending to look after some blockade-runners, when four or five of Blumenburg's thugs picked us up, supposing we were deserters or else persons come to invade their territory. They were going to do all sorts of things to us and pulled out their revolvers. I made no parade of mine though my hand was on it all the time. I quietly informed them of their error, and promised them, each and every one of them, to give them a chance to "play checkers with their noses," and I kept my word, for within a short time I caught them in their nefarious treatment of honest soldiers.

The party was composed of "Boney" Lee, Bob Miller, —— Fletcher, and two others, each one was known to have "done time," yet Blumenburg licensed them. I broke it all up, and they became as meek as lambs.

U. S. Marine Corps

Office Provost Marshal,
8th Army Corps.
Baltimore, Jany. 26, 1865.

STATEMENT OF JAMES BRIERS, LATE OF RICHMOND, VIRGINIA, WHO SAYS:

I am a native of England, came to this country about 1853, remained in Baltimore, Md., about six months then went to Richmond, and went into the employ of the Virginia Central Railroad Co., and remained with them up to this time.

"About December, 1863, I was sent into Lancaster County, by the Railroad Company, to buy pork for them. I remained about three weeks, bought a great many hogs.

November 20th, 1864, was again appointed agent to buy hogs for the Railroad Company, and was sent to Lancaster, Westmorland and other Counties, where I bought about one hundred and fifty head in Lancaster and Richmond Counties, and then returned to Richmond on night of 25th of December.

I was sent back about January 9th, 1865, into the same Counties, to buy pork. Then having a chance to escape I made my way to Westmorland Court House, and there crossed the river into Maryland.

I stopped with Harvey, who keeps the tavern at the Court House, and who has a boat, with which he runs the blockade. John J. Spaulding, a blockade runner, keeps a store at the Court House; he runs over a great many goods; comes over twice a week for goods.

I came over with Spaulding. He thought I was coming over

on business for the Railroad Company, and he was to have his boat over for me, and some goods, in two days' time. I was to be in the neighbourhood of Caywood's place; he, Caywood, was recommended to me as all right. Spaulding charged me fifty dollars in gold and was to bring me back. Gilson, a blockade runner, came over with me.

He is a noted blockade runner, and he is in this city now. He ships his goods from here by vessel, marked to New York. The vessel on the way puts out the goods; I have seen the goods. A Confederate Captain also came over with me; he intended to get a boat and cross the Bay to the Eastern shore of Maryland, on a visit.

Watkins and Pumphrey, two blockade runners at the Court House, also run the blockade on a large scale; also a man by the name of Hayden.

Dr. Spaulding, a brother of John J. Spaulding, came over a few days since and took his wife over the river with him; she lived near Leonardtown.

Judge Irving, Captain Thomas, and Fred. Smith, an old blockade firm on the lower river, are still in that business, with the exception of Smith, who was captured by Colonel Woolley with a large lot of tobacco, and now said to be in Fort McHenry.

Their goods are marked for New York, and landed down the Bay, so Gibson says, and then run to Smith's Point Light-house, to a man called James Sutton, who lives on the Virginia shore of the creek running between Smith's Point and the Virginia shore.

Bows, Wells, Hayden and Pumphrey, a party of blockade runners, have a plan laid to bring over to the father of a late Confederate soldier, living in St. Mary's County, a noted horse upon which the son was killed in battle; they are to come over the first dark night when the ice gives away in Poor Jack Creek.

The names of the blockade runners I know are J. J. Spaulding, Dr. Eck Spaulding, Frank Simms, Warren, Hayden, Bowers, Wells, Watkins, Pumphrey, Harvey.

The blockade runners generally sink their boats in the creek, when not in use.

(Sworn and subscribed.)

460 15th Street,
Washington, D. C.
Feb. 3, 1865.

Lt. Smith,

Chief of Detectives.

Sir.—I desire to call your attention to the cases of Bollman, Mc-Guarty, Welsh and another, privates in the U. S. Marine Corps, wherein I submitted affidavits to you some weeks since.

Their commanding officer has once or twice enquired of me what disposition had been made of their matter. I told him that I had in accordance with the instructions of Colonel Woolley, submitted the papers to you and that you had told me they would be attended to in due course of business. He is, however, very anxious to have the matter disposed of as soon as possible, as the men are at any moment liable to be detailed on distant duty.

If you will, kindly inform me, as soon as practicable, what determination you have come to in these cases.

Very respy.,

Selden Hetzel,

Attorney at Law.

I cannot recall the cases.

General W. W. Morris in Command

To make himself familiar with the work in the departments, he interviewed the heads; finally he wanted to see me. He made the call pleasant by saying: "I hear your work well spoken of," for which I of course thanked him. I told him I had been Assistant Provost Marshal under him at Fort McHenry. The old soldier brightened up and re-marked: "Oh, yes, now I remember; my Adjutant General blamed you for all his troubles. Do you think Andrews was wrong?" I answered: "Yes, he ought to have worn the grey."

Not many days after, I received a telegram from General Sheridan, directing the arrest and confinement of E. W. Andrews, captain, and formerly Assistant Adjutant General.

Believing that if Andrews was in Baltimore he would first call on General Morris, I went there at once, and showed the General the telegram. Very soon Andrews, with his usual pomp, came in. He espied me at once. I showed him my authority from General Sheridan, to arrest him. I permitted him to see General Morris—in my presence, however—and extended him all courtesies I consistently could; finally taking him in a carriage to Fort McHenry, I obtained the following receipt:

Feb. 25, 1865.

Recd. from Captain Wiegel, E. W. Andrews, a prisoner, for safe keeping.

Dan. Macauley,
Col. 11th Ind. Vet. Vols.,
Commanding Brigade.

This receipt was given me in the room formerly occupied by E. W. Andrews, as Adjutant General. What a fall was there!

This was Andrews's exeunt, for I have never seen him since. I subsequently, however, learned of his offense in the Valley. It was more flirting with the enemy. Some of Mosby's men had been captured, and Andrews came to their rescue and vouched for them as being peaceful citizens, upon which they were released, but in a few days they were again captured while committing warlike depredations.

Ordered to New York

Headquarters, Middle Department,
8th Army Corps. Baltimore,
Feby. 10, 1865.

Special Order No. 27.

Lieut. H. B. Smith, 5th N. Y. H. Arty. and Commanding Detectives, Middle Department, 8th Army Corps, with one man,
Lucius Babcock, of his force, will proceed to New York City, on
special government business.

After transacting same, he will at once return to these headquarters.

Quartermasters will furnish transportation.

By command of Bvt. Brigadier General Morris.

Wm. H. Wiegel,
Capt. & Actg. Provost Marshal.

The following refers to my seeking extended territory:

Headquarters, Middle Department,
8th Army Corps.
Baltimore, Feby. 21, 1865.

Unofficial.

Captain:

General Morris desires you to write a letter about Lieut. Smith,
asking such an appointment as will suit him. Address it to the
Adjutant General and send it to me and I will get the General
to put an endorsement on and forward it.

Don't you think you could take it to the Secretary and accomplish something?　　　Yours truly,　Samuel B. Lawrence,

To Capt. Wiegel.　　　Assistant Adjutant General.

Pending the issuance of a commission which was to give me an independent command, to operate in the Shenandoah Valley, and also south of the lower Potomac, I had been striving to get authority to extend our operations to the Rappahannock, to avail ourselves of the valuable data we had accumulated.

Captain Wiegel and I went to Washington, as suggested by Colonel Lawrence, to see Secretary Stanton. When we arrived at Mr. Stanton's door I discovered the mental makeup and character of Wiegel. Mr. Stanton, in manner, was not pleasant to interview. He was brusque, rough, and appeared to think the world was made for him. Wiegel had much *avoirdupois*, but not deep brain convolutions. He had been on General Butler's staff in New Orleans. He was full of egotism, but when he approached Mr. Stanton's door he wilted, and asked me to do the talking, while he listened.

Mr. Stanton did not eat me, and on March 20th our request was granted. I have always found it pleasanter to do business with the proprietor than with the man that sweeps out.

There is no doubt but that Secretary Stanton made many critics by his brusque manner. One did not need to waste words with him, but if a communication was couched in terse language it pleased him. He disliked a cringing interviewer. I did not dislike to have business with him, nor have I ever with men similarly constituted.

Wiegel was a domineering blusterer to his subordinates, but a cringing sycophant to those over him. Stanton's office was not a congenial climate for him.

Secretary Dana was a most agreeable gentleman and no less an executive than Stanton.

Miss Branson Appeared
to Plead For Him

I will now introduce the material from which was builded an actor. Lewis Paine, who brutally hacked at Secretary Seward while Booth was assassinating the President. He was one of the characters produced for the closing scene in that greatest tragedy.

Headquarters, Middle Department,
8th Army Corps.
Baltimore, Mch. 12, 1865.

Major Wm. H. Wiegel,

    Actg. Provost Marshal.

Major.—I have the honour to report the arrest of Lewis Paine, a refugee from Fauquier County, Va.

He was arrested at the house of Miss Maggie Branson, No. 16 North Eutaw Street. She is a noted Rebel.

I was promised evidence to prove that he had been in Baltimore before, but the witnesses are not forthcoming, and I believe him innocent of that charge, but I think it would be well to remove him from that family. I would respectfully recommend his release.

Very respy. your obdt. servt.,
H. B. Smith.
Lt. & Chief.

When I entered my office on Friday morning March 10, 1865, Captain Webb, my clerk, was trying to obtain from Paine some part of his pedigree, but was baffled by the prisoner's dumbness. Then I tried with the result as follows:

Baltimore, Md.,
March 10, 1865

Lewis Paine, refugee from Fauquier County, Virginia, my parents reside near Orleans, in that County. I am eighteen and a half years old. I have not been out of Virginia since the war commenced, until this time.

I was never in the Rebel army. Mosby used to stay at the house of Joe Blackwell, until his house was burned.

Willie Tung, of Warrenton.

Daniel Moffit, of Fauquier County, members of Mosby's command.

Miss Maggie Branson, with whom I was stopping, is related to me by marriage.

I bought the coat and vest of grey cloth in this city, since I came here; my pants of grey I bought in Washington.

I don't remember of hearing any disloyal remarks from any of the boarders at the house No. 16 North Eutaw Street. I whipped a coloured woman at that house on Monday last, because she insulted me; her name is Annie.

(Signed)   L. Paine.

Sworn and subscribed to, before me, this 10th day of March, 1865.

H. B. Smith,
Lt. & Chief.

Paine was a sullen, dumb looking, overgrown young person. To get anything out of him I alternately prodded and fondled; he was a cross between a big booby and a sullen animal.

His statement is disjointed. Between the joints you must imagine my questions, eliciting his words; for instance, "I am eighteen and a half years old," was in reply to my query about his pretensions to never having been in the army. To my remarks about his new grey clothes, certainly pointing their use, where grey was worn, he tried to explain his innocence, etc, etc.

While in the midst of his examination, Miss Branson, accompanied by a Mr. Shriver, came in. Miss Branson pressed right up to my desk, enquiring what charge was against Mr. Paine. She said he was her cousin, and that she knew he had never been north before, etc.

I informed her that her word on such matters was not valuable, since I had her history for disloyalty in my cabinet. I said to Mr. Shriv-

Lewis Paine

er, whom I knew to be reckoned as a loyal man, that he should not have lent his presence.

I was not in good humour because persons who had promised to testify that Paine had been in Baltimore before had failed to respond. I felt in my bones he was a spy, but could not prove it, and therefore could not hold him, hence my recommendation for his release. Finally, on the 12th, he took the oath of allegiance, before me, and I paroled him, inserting in the parole, "to go north of Philadelphia and remain during the war."

After the assassination, this paper was found on Paine, but he had obliterated the restriction "to go north of Philadelphia," etc.

I took from him his pass and parole, issued at Alexandria, Virginia, January 13th, 1865. In it he was described as of dark complexion, black hair, blue eyes, height six feet one and a half inches.

I will now leave Paine until after the assassination, which was just one month later, April 14th, 1865.

I presume my order to go to New York (following) may have hastened my disposition of Paine.

Manahan Involved

Headquarters, Middle Department,
8th Army Corps.
Baltimore, Mch. 12, 1865.

Special Order No. 44.

Lieut. H. B. Smith, 5th N.Y. Arty., and Commanding Detective Corps, 8th Army Corps, with one man of his force, will proceed to New York City, arrest a certain man, and return to these headquarters without delay, with his assistant and prisoner. Quartermaster's Department will furnish transportation.

By command of Bvt. Brigadier General W.W. Morris.

Wm. H. Wiegel,
Major & Actg. Provost Marshal.

The cause for this trip will be explained by the following copy of a letter, and a contract.

New York, Mch. 10, 1865.

Dear Manahan:

It is said Fredericksburg and tobacco is captured. I feared this. Have written to Maddox and sent him a copy of contract. I enclose yours.

Now it is for you to go to work at once and see that this property is taken care of. I believe you will both do it; see to it that no innocent parties suffer. Act promptly, for I assured my friends that the property was safe at that point, and I did it on your representations. Let me hear from you, care of Burnett & Funkhouser, this city.

Yours truly, M. E. Martin.

Baltimore, Md.,

Dec. 8th, 1864.

I hereby agree to deliver to Mess. Maddox & Manahan, during the month of Feby. and March, 1865, at Fredericksburg, Virginia, on the Rappahannock River, Four Thousand Boxes (4,000) of good sound merchantable tobacco, to be paid for on delivery, by my Agents at said point, in United States currency, at the rate of Forty-seven and a half (47½) Cents per pound.

Said tobacco to be of the quality known as good manufactured Virginia Leaf. I reserve to myself the privilege of increasing the quantity to 5,000 boxes, if I see proper.

(Signed)   M. E. Martin.

Manahan was of the firm of J. F. Manahan & Co., No. 17 South Charles Street, Baltimore, Md. This letter, by mistake, fell into my hands on March 12th. It was necessary to act quickly in order to intercept communication twixt Martin and Manahan, and for that purpose I left Baltimore on the 12th, and had my man wire to Martin, as follows:

Baltimore, Md., Mch. 13, 1865.

M. E. Martin,

  c/o Burnett & Funkhouser,

    New York.

Your letter here. Shaffer, my friend, will call today. Let me know the result by telegraph immediately.

Manahan,

Maltby House.

I assumed that if Martin wanted to reach Manahan, he would address him at the Maltby House, the telegraph office there was in my possession.

I at the same time had myself wired to as follows:

Baltimore, Md., Mch. 13, 1865.

I. K. Shaffer,

  Merchants Hotel,

    New York.

Call on Martin immediately, I have his letter of 10th.

Manahan,

Maltby House.

This wire was to be my introduction to Martin. I located Martin and Burnett & Funkhouser in Broad Street near Beaver. I did not call on him immediately, as I wanted him to get anxious to see me first.

To keep him quiet on Maddox, I had him wired as follows:

Washington, D. C.,
Mch. 14, 1865.

M. E. Martin,
 c/o Burnett & Funkhouser,
  New York.
M. leaves here tonight, you can rest fully satisfied all is right.
J. F. Manahan,
Willards Hotel.

Poor Manahan was asleep to all this use of his name, of course. Martin did get anxious. He wrote me the following note and sent it to Merchant's Hotel:

Mr. Shaffer:
Dear Sir.—Have despatch from Manahan that you will call and see me here. Will be in at half past eleven to twelve, half past twelve to one, and at half past one.
Either wait for me or leave your address.
Yours, &c.,
M. E. Martin.

I called but failed to find Martin, and later I received the following from him:

Mr. Shaffer:
I waited for you all the early part of the day, at B & F's, and then left a note for you, requesting you to leave your address.
Am unwell; if it is important you should see me before morning, please come up to my hotel, Gramercy Park House, if not, please meet me at B & F's, nine to nine thirty, t-morrow morning.
Yours truly,
Martin.

I met him in the morning, as appointed. He was hungry to meet me, just as I wanted it.

I found Mr. Martin to be a man evidently well fitted for the job, in appearance tall, rather lank, energetic and gentlemanly. We visited off and on, nearly all day. He believed, from what I told him, that I and my friends were financially interested through Manahan. He explained his position as representing Mr. Trenholm, Secretary of the Confederate Treasury. He told how he had formerly run cotton through the lines on the Mississippi river.

Now that the tobacco had been seized, his plan was to press a claim upon our government, representing the tobacco to belong to Union people. He told me he had papers at his hotel which would corroborate him.

In the afternoon, nearly dark, we parted in the Howard House (then at the corner of Maiden Lane and Broadway) with the understanding that I was returning to Baltimore and Manahan, satisfied with his assurances.

My man (Mr. Kraft), who had been following me, to be handy if help was needed, and who had been watching for the signal to make the arrest, came to me hastily, thinking he might have missed the signal, but I assured him it was all right to let Martin go. I had a further purpose, I wanted to get the documents Martin had spoken of as being at his hotel.

Kraft and I dined at the old Lovejoy Hotel (then at the corner of Beekman Street and Park Row) and afterwards went up to the Gramercy Park Hotel, then quite a fashionable hostelry. We waited until Martin came out of the dining-room. He was in his dinner suit, and was quite a dude for such a raw-boned Southerner; he was surprised to see me again. I told him I wanted some further talk. I asked if we could not go to his room. After starting for up stairs I introduced my friend.

When in his room I informed him that my sole object was to obtain the information needed by the Government. Any man's face would be a study under such circumstances. Martin was game; his first question was: "Well, what is your name?"

"Smith," I replied.

"Oh, I mean your right name," he said. (There are some advantages in the name Smith, I really needed no *alias*.)

Martin thought a treat was "on him," and he paid it. I then invited him to show me the documents he had described when down town. I took possession of all. They gave a very good history of his doings on the Mississippi river, and his connection with the Confederate Treasury Department.

In answer to his question, I told him that I did not know what the government would do with him, but I was sure his proposed claim against the government would not be collectible, and perhaps he would be detained until the end of the war, to prevent a recurrence.

Pending my first call on Martin, I visited General Dix, commanding the Department of the East. He declined to endorse my order to make the arrest of Martin, unless I explained fully the case. Rather than do so, just at that time, I concluded to disregard courtesy and take my man away without his endorsement, which I did.

The "Gold Room" which was then more important than the Stock Exchange, was in Twenty-fourth Street, back of the Fifth Avenue Hotel; it was open evenings. I permitted Martin to send there for money, and to advise his friends that he would be away for a few days.

During the evening Mr. Martin said to me, "Last evening, when I was expecting you, waiting for you, I lay here reading Colonel Baker's book on the Secret Service. He had no case as slick as this. Smith, you were so frank and open, I would have told you anything you wanted to know."

I presume he was reading Baker's book to see how such cases as his were treated, not dreaming of an ocular demonstration so near at hand. At midnight we started for Baltimore.

The following from the Richmond *Whig* explains better, perhaps, than I can, just what Martin and the case meant, from the Confederate viewpoint:

(FROM THE RICHMOND *WHIG*)

The Tobacco Transaction—A Prominent New York House Concerned.

We have obtained the main facts of the great tobacco speculation, in reference to which there were so many rumours last week. It appears that an agent of a New York mercantile house, whose name it is deemed inexpedient to publish at this time, proposed to certain parties in this city to contract with them for the delivery of a specific quantity of manufactured tobacco at Fredericksburg, he undertaking for his principals to remove the tobacco from that point, with the implied consent of the United States authorities, provided the Confederate authorities would indicate their consent, in writing, to the proposed transaction. The tobacco was to be paid for on its delivery at Fredericksburg. The New York house was vouched for by an influential member of Congress, who had intimate business relations with the concern.

One of the Confederate bureaus became identified with the scheme, by reason of the representations which had been made to its officers, and by the prospect of advantageous results from the fulfilment of the proposed agreement by the parties on the other side.

The contract was accordingly entered into, "sealed, signed and delivered," with a satisfactory endorsement from the predecessor of the present Secretary of War, who was no doubt induced to believe that it was "all right." Nothing was said in the contract about bacon. The *quid pro quo* was money.

In execution of the contract on this side, about four thousand boxes of fine to extra manufactured tobacco were purchased here, at rates ranging from four dollars to seven dollars per pound, Confederate currency. Of this amount one thousand two hundred and seventy-three boxes, weighing one hundred and thirty-two thousand five hundred and seventy-eight pounds, and valued at seven hundred thousand dollars, were forwarded to Fredericksburg in charge of Dr. Rose, who was induced by assurances from Richmond, which he could not discredit, to act as consignee and custodian of the tobacco until delivered according to agreement. He was not in any sense, as we understand, a party to the contract. What became of the tobacco is known to our readers. Dr. Rose was carried off by the Yankees for engaging in contraband traffic.

The name of General Singleton has been connected with this transaction. We state on the authority of an officer of the bureau referred to that he has no lot nor part in it, directly or indirectly. The loss of the tobacco will fall upon the contractors here unless the New York parties to the contract will fulfil their obligations by indemnifying the bureau with which they contracted.

After action by Congress, President Lincoln endeavoured to extend some relief to persons within the Confederacy who were Unionists at heart; they were to be encouraged by allowing them to work their products up to and through the lines. What was intended as a great beneficent proposition was seized upon by the Confederate government to help itself financially.

The following order will explain the experiences with cotton on the Mississippi River. I presume these orders drove Martin to turn his attention to tobacco in the east:

> Headquarters, Major General Washburn,
> District West Tennessee.
> Memphis, May 10, 1864.

The practical operation of commercial intercourse from this city with the States in rebellion, has been to help largely to feed, clothe, arm and equip our enemies.

To take cotton, belonging to the Rebel Government to Memphis, and convert it into supplies and greenbacks, and return to the lines of the enemy, or place the proceeds to the credit of the Rebel Government, in Europe, is safe and easy.

I have undoubted evidence that large amounts of cotton have been and are being brought here to be sold, belonging to the Rebel Government.

It is therefore ordered, that on and after the 15th of May, 1864, the lines of the Army at Memphis be closed and no person be permitted to leave the city, except by river, without a special pass.

> By order of
> Major General C. C. Washburn.

A similar order was issued by Colonel Farrar, at Natchez, Miss., and by General Sherman at Vicksburg, in which they said:

The amount of trade through the lines at all these points, with the isolated localities, where trade stores were situated, was estimated at not less than a half million dollars, daily.

On the 6th of March, 1864, General Roberts, with one thousand five hundred men, and with naval help, left Fortress Monroe for Fredericksburg. He captured and destroyed three hundred and eighty thousand dollars worth of tobacco.

Martin was the representative of the Confederate Treasury Department. I recovered his correspondence with Secretary Trenholm. It was understood that the proceeds of the sale of this tobacco was to go to Paris to help pay Confederate debts incurred there.

A Kidnapped Coloured Boy

Headquarters, Middle Department,
8th Army Corps.
Baltimore, Mch. 18, 1865.

Lieut. Smith:

I want to see you at the office this evening at 7.30.

The Secretary of War wants to see you in Washington, and you will have to go tomorrow morning.

Yours, &c.,
S. B. Lawrence,
A. Adjutant General.

I do not remember what the Secretary wanted, but as the following order issued the next day, I assume it was to learn more of my purpose in the extended territory asked for:

War Department,
Washington, D. C.,
Mch. 20, 1865.

Major W. H. Wiegel:

Provost Marshal at Baltimore is authorized to extend his operations into the region between the Potomac and Rappahannock Rivers known as the northern neck of Virginia.

(Signed)   C. A. Dana,
Asst. Secretary of War.

Headquarters, Department of Missouri,
Office of Provost Marshal General,
St. Louis, Mo., Mch. 21, 1865.

Provost Marshal General,
Middle Department,
Baltimore, Md.

Sir.—In October last, the Military Prisons of this city being in danger from the Rebel forces under Major General Sterling Price, it was deemed prudent by General Rosecrans, then in command of this Department, to transfer the occupants to the Alton Prison. While this transfer was in progress, one of the prisoners, Robert Loudan, *alias* Charles Veal, made his escape from the guards by cutting his irons and jumping from the boat into the river. He was then under sentence of death for being a spy and a boat burner.

Loudan was lately heard from at New Orleans, where it was reported he was in the custody of the Military authorities, by whom he was subsequently released for the want of sufficient evidence to hold him.

It is possible he has gone beyond our lines, but, if not, he would be likely to make for some of the large cities of the loyal States.

Loudan is a native of Philadelphia, where his wife now resides; height, about five feet eight inches; complexion, fair; large blue eyes constantly rolling and displaying a great deal of white; hair and whiskers, fair; square shoulders; usually wears a false moustache; wears his hat on the back of his head.

This office is charged with his execution, and will incur any amount of trouble to recapture him. If he is found within the limits of your jurisdiction, please secure and forward him to me or notify me of his arrest and I will send for him.

Very respectfully, Your obdt. servt.,
J. H. Baker, Col. & Provost Marshal.

Headquarters, Middle Department,
8th Army Corps.
Baltimore, Mch. 31, 1865.

Special Order No. 55.

Lieut. H. B. Smith, 5th N. Y. H. Arty., Commanding Detective Corps, Middle Department, 8th Army Corps, will proceed to Washington, D. C., for the recovery of a coloured boy, kidnapped from Norfolk, Virginia, and will report to the Provost Marshal of Washington, for any assistance he may require.

By command of Bvt. Brigadier General W. W. Morris.

Wm. H. Wiegel,

Major & Actg. Provost Marshal.

File 39

Captain Fitzhugh

Headquarters, Middle Department,
8th Army Corps.
Baltimore, Apl. 5, 1865.

Major:

I have written to Commodore Dornin requesting him to send a small steamer in pursuit of the *Harriet Deford*, if he has one ready, and to permit Lieut. Smith and his guard to accompany her.

If Commodore Dornin cannot send a steamer I have written to Colonel Newport, to request him to place a tug at your disposal.

You will please see that Smith goes in Command with sufficient guard and ammunition. If you want a Howitzer, send to C. O. Fort McHenry, or let the steamer stop there and get it.

Very respy. your obdt. servt.,
Samuel B. Lawrence,
A. Adjutant General.

To Major Wiegel.

Commandant's Office.
Naval Station,
Baltimore, Apl. 5, 1865.

Colonel:

I regret that I have no steamer in the proper condition to start off; if we had it would be furnished promptly.

Very respy. your obdt. servt,

To   Thos A. Dornin, Commodore.

Col. Sam'l B. Lawrence, A. Adjutant General, Middle Department.

A report had reached us that the steamer *Harriet Deford*, plying between the Patuxent River and Baltimore, had been captured by a gang of pirates, in Fair Haven Bay, which is midway between the Patuxent River and the Severn River; the passengers were robbed and put ashore.

Richmond had fallen; Jefferson Davis was seeking to escape, and the theory, quickly arrived at, was that this steamer had been seized to furnish the means, perhaps, to run him to the Bahamas, or Bermuda.

The bay and its tributaries were alive with anxiety. In a very short time I was away in a tug. I put the guards below decks, in the coal-hole, where they were nearly smothered, until night came on.

Early in the evening we arrived at the mouth of Fair Haven Bay. Our pilot did not know the harbour, but soon discovered he could not run his boat on the mere appearance of water. He ran us onto a bar, where we thumped and thumped, backed and poled off, and then ran onto another. We finally concluded to back off, go back to the Severn River and Annapolis, and wait for daylight.

When we arrived in the Severn, we found the shore and water full of alertness. We were hailed and threatened until our character was understood. To my delight I found there a large steamer, with two hundred men on, that Colonel Lawrence had sent down to support me. A landlubber feels better on a larger vessel, so I took my men on the steamer, and we started again for Fair Haven. We arrived there early in the morning.

My theory was that I could pick up some clue there to follow up, and events sustained me. I sauntered up from the dock towards a store. I met two men, and to my question, one of the men admitted he was pressed into service by the gang in the mouth of the Patuxent. He said the party had crossed the Potomac in a small sail boat, and compelled him to pilot them, to overhaul the *Harriet Deford*. He said they steamed down the bay, after leaving Fair Haven. We held him, and at once ran on down the Chesapeake, to the mouth of the Potomac. We were then in Commodore Parker's territory, which he was covering clear across the bay with gunboats. Our duty was done, and we returned to Baltimore.

I learned afterwards that they ran the *Deford* into Mobjack Bay, where she was burned, after first stripping her joiner work. I visited, and afterwards married, Aunt Mag, in the region of Mobjack Bay, but never referred to the incident. I thought it might not bring up pleasant recollections. I have often wondered if some of the *Deford's* saloon trimmings might be in use in some of the houses there. Let us forget it.

The following account of the affair appeared in the New York papers under date April 6th, 1865, with big headline: "*Another Pirate!*"

"Baltimore, April 5th, 1865. A daring act of piracy was perpetrated at Fair Haven, Herring Bay, about fifty miles from this city, the Steamer *Harriet Deford* being seized by a company of Rebel soldiers in disguise. The *Deford* had scarcely left Fair Haven Wharf before a dozen or more of newly received passengers threw off their overcoats and drawing revolvers revealed to the astonished gaze of the passengers the uniforms of Rebel soldiers.

The passengers, about seventy in number, thirty being ladies, were ordered to the saloon and guards placed over them while the balance of the pirates proceeded to take command of the Steamer. Captain and officers were forced into obedience at the muzzle of the pirates' revolvers. One of the pirates assumed control of the wheel, the Pilot and Engineer being compelled to proceed to sea. Mr. A. Donnell, clerk of the *Deford*, believing that he had met the leader of the outlaws on a former occasion, accosted him as Captain Fitzhugh, when the latter acknowledged the recognition and said he was Captain of the Fifth Virginia Cavalry and acting under orders of superior officers. Under the persuasive eloquence of a revolver the clerk handed over to the pirates nearly twelve hundred dollars belonging to the owners of the Steamer and different firms in this City; which Fitzhugh carefully robbed.

When about a mile from Fair Haven, Fitzhugh compelled the Engineer to sound the steam whistle three times, in answer to which signal three boats containing thirty-two men put off from each side of the river and stood for the Steamer. The crews of these boats having been taken aboard, the Steamer was headed down Chesapeake Bay. On the way down Captain Leage, Captain Dayton, officer in charge of the Steamer and several old gentlemen with ladies and children, were placed on board of the Schooner *Hiawatha*, bound for this city. The balance of male passengers, Engineer, Fireman, and twenty coloured freedmen were retained as prisoners.

The *Deford* was valued at fifty thousand dollars and had a cargo of tobacco, potatoes, grain, furs, &c., valued at eighty thousand dollars. Fitzhugh would not permit his men to rob passengers.

The captured Steamer is a fast sailer, having repeatedly made fourteen knots per hour. The intention of the pirates could not be learned, but it is supposed they will endeavour to run outside the Capes, transfer the cargo to a larger vessel, burn the *Deford*, and proceed to Nassau.

The paroled passengers arrived here this morning. One of them positively asserts that Jeff. Davis was among the party who came out in small boats, but no reliance whatever can be placed in the possibility of Jeff. having thus escaped from Richmond. The receipt of this news caused great excitement here, and measures looking to the defence of the Bay boats are being made.

A steamer has also been despatched to intercept the pirates before they reach the Capes."

Ordered to Northern Neck of Virginia

At this time in 1865 General Lee was about surrendering. All the people, North and South, were rejoicing at the prospect of peace, excepting those bitter, poisoned-with-their-own-venom conspirators hid away in dark corners, who were rehearsing for the closing scene.

> Headquarters, Middle Department,
> 8th Army Corps.
> Baltimore, Apl. 13, 1865.

Special Order No. 61.

1st Lieut. H. B. Smith, in accordance with instructions received from the Hon. Secretary of War, will proceed to that part of Virginia known as the Northern Neck, with two of his men, and prisoner, M. V. B. Morgan, for the purpose of arresting certain outlaws in that part of Virginia.

Military and Naval commanders will please give all assistance required.

> By command of Bvt. Brigadier General W. W. Morris.
> Wm. H. Wiegel,
> Major & Actg. Provost Marshal.

This was to be my first opportunity to set foot in the district I had been seeking to. I had intended to capture in detail every known blockade-runner, and lock them up until the end of the war, but now that the war was practically over, my purpose was to capture the contraband goods to be found hidden in hay stacks, barns, etc.

Martin Van Buren Morgan had been with these blockade-runners, and had himself been somewhat in their ways, so I had become satisfied he would serve me, for pay. An order was placed in my hands, to be used under certain conditions. If he proved loyal and valuable, it was not to be used. If he was not valuable, I could use it and send him north. If he proved disloyal, I had verbal instructions to use my own judgment as to his disposal. This was the order:

Headquarters, Middle Department,
8th Army Corps.
Baltimore, Apl. 13, 1865.

Special Order No. 61.

2—M. V. B. Morgan, citizen prisoner, is hereby ordered to proceed north of Philadelphia, Pa., and remain during the war, provided he takes the oath of allegiance to the United States Government.

By command of Bvt. Brigadier General W. W. Morris.
Wm. H. Wiegel,
Major & Actg. Provost Marshal.

MORGAN'S STATEMENT

My name is Martin Van Buren Morgan. I was born in Palmyra, New York State. My father was named Irvin Morgan, my brother is named Francis Morgan. My father one year ago was in Nashville, Tenn. I was so young I cannot remember when I lived in Palmyra; as far back as I can recollect I was in Oswego. When three years old we moved to Cleveland, Ohio. When about sixteen I moved to Wheeling with my mother. From Wheeling I ran on the river from Cincinnati to Pittsburg.

In November, 1860, I was in Cleveland, Ohio. I voted for Abraham Lincoln. From Cleveland I went to Cincinnati, to Pittsburg, and then to Queen's County, Virginia, in January, 1861.

On March 4th, 1861, I was still in Queen's County, Virginia. I did not vote in Virginia. Mr. Thompson took me to Virginia. I never belonged to any regiment in the South. I lived in Queen's County until last spring, lived there all the time. I worked there at farming and oystering. I own a little place of about ten acres. I worked for Mr. Richardson and Captain Baggs.

Since last spring I have been living in Westmorland and Northumberland Counties. They ran me away from Queen's County. I lived near Union, in Northumberland. I used to oyster on the Wicomico River, &c.

When the raid was made last June, on the Necks, I was there.

They did not find my boat that I oyster with, as it was hauled up and covered with pine boughs. I remained hid. I saw a few coloured soldiers. Have seen conscripting officers and I always ran away from them. Have never been to Richmond since 1861.

I sent a letter by George Booth across the river and heard from my father the same way. The carrier who works from Rap ——— to Potomac, is named James Wilds; I don't know the points he stops at. Charles or George Booth carries the mail across the Potomac.

I addressed the letter I sent to my father to Nashville, Tenn. I have a brother in the Southern army; he belongs to the fourth Georgia regiment; he is a Captain. I received an answer to the letter I sent my father. I never wrote to him again, and have had no letter from him since.

I left Northumberland County last August, and crossed over to the Maryland side. I came across in an oyster punt, at night. The boat belonged to me. I came over alone, brought nothing with me; landed on the Maryland side, at the barns, near Marshal's store, on the St. George's Island. Bennett and King live there.

When I landed on the Maryland side, I saw Ben. King, Bennett, and Mr. Snyder, who all came to the barn. I went over to Maryland to get shoes and to dredge, but could get no work and had to come back. I also got some sugar; I got Ben. King to get it for me. I got one pair of shoes, one pound of coffee and one pound of sugar. This is all I could get. I paid five dollars for the shoes, seventy-five cents for the coffee and thirty cents for the sugar. I bought these things for Mrs. Kent: I was living with her. King has been driven off the Island. I stayed in Maryland a week and then paddled back to old Virginia, to old Virginia shore.

About the 1st September I came to Maryland shore again, paddled over on a dark night, brought nothing over with me, again landed at the same place. I came over for stuff. Pickets were on the shore and I could not land, and had to put back. I carried over forty dollars in greenbacks.

After about a week I went over again, taking over the same thing; nothing. I landed this time at Chicken Cock, above Smith's Creek, a *leetle*. I got my goods at Mr. Bean's. Mr. Bean keeps a store. I got a pair of boots for eight dollars, one pair pants for five dollars, one fine-tooth comb for fifteen cents, and also a bottle of hair oil at thirty or forty cents, and had three or four glasses of whiskey.

I treated a lieutenant and a captain who were there from Piney Point. I had to lay in the bushes about two days, the weather being so rough I could not cross. I spent about thirty dollars.

On last Monday night I came over again; came over alone, and in a canoe worth one hundred and fifty dollars; left the canoe on the beach. I bought this canoe about a week before I came over. I bought this canoe to run the blockade with. I was going to run Jews across for Mr. Dawson. Mr. Dawson lives at the head of Large Creek, Yocomico River. Colonel Claybrook, of Home Guard, lives on the road from Large Creek to Union Village.

I saw in Northumberland County about three months since, Albert Klockgether, who gave me his address in Baltimore, and desired me, when I came over, to call and see him. Bill Hayden carried over Klockgether, in one of Dawson's boats.

I left my boat near Britton's Bay, on the beach. Bill Hayden has been captured twice, and is now back in Virginia. I came to this city on the West River boat, and landed this afternoon. I bought this shirt I have on from Mr. Wm. Hudson, a blockade runner; paid him six dollars for it about three or four weeks since. I have heard that Hudson is now captured. Bought my hat for five dollars from the same one. I bought my satchel from Richard King, a blockade runner. I bought the revolver from a Jew in Virginia; paid twenty dollars for it.

A man named Brown is a blockade runner. I heard that he brought over a load of Enfield rifles, in a sloop; the Home Guard are armed with them.

A Jew named Rosenfield is connected between Wilmington and Canada and England, in running the blockade. A woman named Mrs. Hays, of Baltimore, was with Rosenfield; she had a trunk and satchel; she came over to Dawson's. She was coming from Richmond.

Rosenfield said he was going back. I knew three Jews by sight, who have brought medicine across—I think from Eastern shore. I don't know their names.

A Rebel officer, Captain Berry, came over to the Maryland side in full uniform, and came back again. I have seen him lots of times; he is stationed above Boler's, who lives at the ferry over the Rappahannock, about twenty miles from mouth of the river.

They have large flat boats to carry over men, oxen, wagons, &c.—have two there now. This ferry is about fifty miles from Richmond. There is a large camp of Cavalry about eight miles from the ferry on the south side of the river. Gunboats can come up as far as Boler's. Captain Moon lives opposite the guard ship, on the Virginia side, at the windmill.

Foster Maynard took the oath at Point Lookout, and is now conscript officer; he is a Captain. Maynard lives about one mile from King's Sail. King's Sail is on the Yocomico River.

About two weeks since, Bill Hayden and Joe Cooper came over to Britton's Bay, to a little creek this side of the Bay, just above Piney Point; a white house is on the shore. The house right by the saw mill is the house they go to. They go to this house to buy goods to run the blockade with. I bought a little cutter from this place; bought over three sacks of salt, hats, caps, boots, shoes, and a jug of whiskey.

Richard King, of Northumberland County, a blockade runner, comes to this side of the river and buys canoes and yawl boats. King has been over here for the last three weeks. About four weeks ago King got a canoe from Alexandria, and took it over to Dawson's and sold it to him. He came to Baltimore once, on a *pungy*.

John Olison owns a *pungy*; dredges around St. George's. He lives on the Virginia side. Elias Steele, blockade runner, lives in Westmorland County. Captain Wm. Dawson lives at Large Creek.

Union Village is where the mail comes. It comes every week (not certain). Mrs. Frank Lewis gave me the letter addressed to Mr. Steele, to give to Mr. Steele. (I never gave it to him.) Union Village is about eight miles from the beach. I found out that Mr. Steele had crossed the Potomac.

I have seen large quantities of tobacco hid under corn shucks, and I know he has a large sum of money and a number of watches in his house (Dawson's house).

At Dawson's house are the following persons: Mr. Dawson, Sr., Mrs. Dawson, Miss Dawson, Mrs. Nancy Clarke and her daughter, and Dawson, Jr. (a boy).

There are two canoes at Dawson's.

Paine Hung

The saddest day in our nation's history was Friday, April 14th, 1865. Early in the evening I was introduced to General Grant, in his private car; he was on his way from Washington to Philadelphia. The private car was standing on Howard just north of Camden Street. At that time the cars of through trains were hauled through Baltimore by horses up Howard, down Pratt to President Street, and to the depot.

Mr. Wm. G. Woodside, the paymaster of the Baltimore and Ohio Railroad, had asked me if I would like to be introduced to the General. We entered the car from the rear door. I do not remember there being any person in the car except the General and Mrs. Grant. It was understood in Washington that General Grant was to have accompanied the President to the theatre that evening.

We retired at about 10 o'clock, prepared to start the next morning, Saturday, the 15th, for the northern neck of Virginia, with Morgan, as outlined in the file preceding. Soon after retiring we were informed of the assassination. There is no word in the language to describe the shock I felt. I put on my clothes and did not take them off again until Wednesday, the 19th. Adjutant General Lawrence sent for me, and instructed me to abandon my trip to the Northern Neck.

The following telegram came early Saturday morning; in it Paine is described quite perfectly, but at that time I had no idea that he was the person described:

United States Military Telegram,
Apl. 15, 1865.

The following is a description of the assassin of the Hon. W. H. Seward, Secretary of State, and Hon. Frederick W. Seward, Assistant Secretary. You will use every exertion in your power and call to your aid the entire force under your control to secure the arrest of the assassin.

Height 6½ feet, black hair, thick, full, and straight. No beard, nor appearance of beard. Cheeks red on the jaws, and face moderately full. 22 or 23 years of age. Eyes, colour not known, large eyes, not prominent. Brows not heavy, but dark. Face not large, but rather round. Complexion healthy. Nose straight and well formed. Medium sized mouth, small lip, thin upper lip, protrudes when he talks. Chin pointed and prominent. Head of medium size. Neck short and of medium length. Hands small and fingers tapering, showed no signs of hard labour. Broad shoulders, taper waist, straight figure, strong looking man; manner not gentlemanly, but vulgar.

Overcoat double breasted, colour mixed of pink and grey spots, small; was a sack overcoat, pockets inside and on breast, with lapels or flaps. Pants, black, common stuff. New heavy boots. Voice small, inclined to tenor.

(Signed) N. S. Jeffries,
A. P. M. G.

Headquarters, Middle Department,
8th Army Corps.
Baltimore, Apl. 16, 1865.

Colonel:

I have some important intelligence, send Lieut. Smith to me at once.

Samuel B. Lawrence,
A. A. G.

To Colonel Woolley.

The information was about a letter that had been found in Booth's trunk, written from Hookstown, Md., from Samuel Arnold, showing his (Arnold's) complicity in the assassination.

I at once, with one of my men, Mr. Babcock, went to Hookstown. We avoided our pickets, travelled across country, and reached Arnold's home about noon. We sat down, as if to rest, on Arnold's porch, asking no questions, but waited to be questioned. A coloured woman opened the door, and I asked her if she would give us something to eat, for money. She agreed and invited us into the sitting room, while she prepared something for us.

There was no white person about. We ate and visited, she ques-

SAMUEL B. ARNOLD

tioning us about the murder, and we cautioning her. Finally, when we were about to leave, we told her we knew Mr. Arnold. She said he had gone away some days since to Old Point Comfort. Our purpose was accomplished. It is not necessary to say we hurried.

Everybody bound for Old Point had to get a pass at our office. A record was kept of each, together with the name of a person as reference. An examination of the register disclosed at once Samuel B. Arnold's name, vouched for by Mr. Wharton ("Wickey" Wharton), whom we knew; he was sutler at Old Point. We wired to him to know where Arnold was. He replied: "A clerk in my employ." We then wired for his arrest.

He was arrested and sent to Baltimore on the Bay Line boat, reaching Baltimore on the 18th.

The following was my order to go to Washington with him:

Headquarters, Middle Department,
8th Army Corps.

Office Provost Marshal,
 Baltimore, Apl. 18, 1865.
Lieut. H. B. Smith (in citizen's clothes) and officer Babcock, will accompany the officer in charge of S. B. Arnold, to Washington, to aid in securing Arnold's safe delivery. The duty performed they will return to these headquarters without delay.

 By command of Bvt. Brigadier General Morris.

John Woolley,
Lt. Col. Chf. Staff Prov. Mar.

Arnold was sentenced to Dry Tortugas for life. Following is a copy of Arnold's letter, found in Booth's trunk:

Hookstown, Baltimore County, Md.,
March 27, 1865.

Dear John:

Was business so important that you could not remain in Baltimore till I saw you? I came in as soon as I could, but found you had gone to W———n. I called also to see Mike, but learned from his mother he had gone out with you, and had not returned. I concluded, therefore, he had gone with you.

How inconsiderate you have been. When I left you, you stated we would meet in a month or so. Therefore I made application for employment, an answer to which I shall receive during the week. I told my parents I had ceased with you.

Can I then, under existing circumstances, come as you request-ed? You know full well that the G——t suspicions something is going on there; therefore the undertaking is becoming more complicated. Why not, for the present desist, for various rea-sons? which, if you look into, you can readily see without my making any mention thereof to you. Nor anyone can censure me for my present course. You have been its cause, for how can I now come after telling them I had left you? Suspicion rests on me now, from my whole family, and even parties in the country. I will be compelled to leave home, anyhow, and how soon I care not.

None, no, not one, were more in favour of the enterprise than myself, and today would be there, had you not done as you have—by this, I mean, manner of proceeding.

I am, as you well know, in need. I am, you may say, in rags, whereas today I ought to be well clothed.

I do not feel right stalking about without means, and more from appearance a beggar. I feel my independence; but even all this would be, and was forgotten, for I was one with you. Time more propitious will arrive yet. Do not act rashly or in haste. I would prefer your first query, "Go and see how it will be taken at R——d," and ere long I shall be better prepared to again be with you. I dislike writing; would sooner verbally make known my views, yet you know writing causes me thus to proceed.

Do not in anger peruse this, weigh all I have said, and as a rational man and a friend, you cannot censure or upbraid my conduct. I sincerely trust this, nor naught else that shall or may occur, will ever be an obstacle to obliterate our former friend-ship and attachment.

Write me to Baltimore, as I expect to be in about Wednesday or Thursday, or, if you can possibly come on, I will Tuesday meet you in Baltimore at B——. Ever I subscribe myself,

Your friend,
Sam.

Notwithstanding the opprobrium attaching to the name, Arnold, in American history, I have always looked upon this Arnold with some feelings of pity.

The following account of Paine's arrest is borrowed from Mr. Os-born H. Oldroyd's *Assassination of Abraham Lincoln*:

The doorbell of Mrs. Surratt's house, No. 541 (now No. 604) H Street, N.W., was rung by Major H.W. Smith, in company with other officers, about eleven o'clock Monday night, the 17th. When the bell rang, Mrs. Surratt appeared at the window and said: "Is that you, Mr. Kirby"? The reply was that it was not Mr. Kirby, and to open the door.

She opened the door, and was asked: "Are you Mrs. Surratt?" She said: "I am the widow of John H. Surratt."

The officer added, "And the mother of John H. Surratt, Jr.?" She replied: "I am."

Major Smith said: "I come to arrest you and all in your house, and take you for examination to General Augur's headquarters." No inquiry whatever was made as to the cause of arrest. Mr. R. C. Morgan, in the service of the War Department, made his appearance at the Surratt house a few minutes later, sent under orders to superintend the seizure of papers and the arrest of the inmates. While the officers were in the house a knock and ring were heard at the door, and Mr. Morgan and Captain Wermerskirch stepped forward and opened the door, and Lewis Payne stepped in with a pickax over his shoulder, dressed in a gray coat and vest and black trousers.

As he had left his hat in the house of Secretary Seward, he had made one out of the sleeve of a shirt or the leg of a drawers, pulling it over his head like a turban. He said he wished to see Mrs. Surratt, and when asked what he came that time of night for, he replied he came to dig a gutter, as Mrs. Surratt had sent for him in the morning. When asked where he boarded, he said he had no boarding house, that he was a poor man, who got his living with the pick. Mr. Morgan asked him why he came at that hour of the night to go to work? He said he simply called to find out what time he should go to work in the morning.

When asked if he had any previous acquaintance with Mrs Surratt, he answered, "No," but said that she knew he was working around the neighbourhood and was a poor man, and came to him. He gave his age as twenty, and was from Fauquier County, Virginia, and pulled out an oath of allegiance, and on it was "Lewis Payne, Fauquier County, Virginia."

Mrs. Surratt was asked whether she knew him, and she declared in the presence of Payne, holding up her hands: "Before God, I have never seen that man before; I have not hired him; I do not know anything about him."

Mrs. Surratt said to Mr. Morgan: "I am so glad you officers came here tonight, for this man came here with a pickax to kill us."

From Mrs. Surratt's house Payne was taken to the provost marshal's office. Mrs. Surratt was informed that the carriage was ready to take her to the provost marshal's office, and she, with her daughter Annie, Miss Honora Fitzpatrick, and Miss Olivia Jenkins (the latter two boarded at the house), were driven away.

The telegram received on Saturday morning the 15th, giving a description of the person who tried to kill Secretary Seward, was quite accurate, considering it was made by persons under great excitement. The oath of allegiance which Paine pulled out of his pocket when arrested, was the document issued from our office. He had erased, however, the restriction which ordered that he was to "go north of Philadelphia and remain during the war."

Before telling of what I did after discovering Paine to be the person I had released on March 14th, I want you to read the account Mr. Oldroyd gives of his clumsily brutal attack on Secretary Seward:

Lewis Payne (his real name was Lewis Thornton Powell), boarded at the Horndon House, corner Ninth and F Streets, where the Loan and Trust Building now stands, for two weeks, leaving there on the afternoon of April 14th. He paid his bill at four o'clock, and requested dinner before the regular time, and it was served to him.

Very little is known of his whereabouts from that time until 10 p. m., when he rang the bell of the Seward mansion, which stood on the ground now occupied by the Lafayette Opera House.

When the door was opened by the coloured doorkeeper, Payne stepped in, holding a little package in his hand, saying that he had some medicine for Secretary Seward, sent by Dr. Verdi, which he was directed to deliver in person and give instructions how it was to be taken.

The doorkeeper informed him that he could not see Mr. Seward, but he repeated the words, saying he must see him. He talked very roughly for several minutes against the protest of the doorkeeper, who said he had positive orders to admit no one to the sick-chamber.

The doorkeeper finally weakened, thinking perhaps he was sent by Dr. Verdi, and let him ascend the stairs. When at the top, he met Mr. Frederick Seward, a son of the Secretary's to whom he told the object of his visit, but Mr. Seward told him that he could not see his father; that he was asleep, but to give him the medicine and he would take it to him. That would not do; he must see Mr. Seward; and then Mr. Seward said: "I am the proprietor here, and his son; if you cannot leave your message with me, you cannot leave it at all."

Payne started downstairs, and after taking a few steps, suddenly turned around and struck Mr. Frederick Seward, felling him to the floor. Sergeant George F. Robinson, acting as attendant nurse to Mr. Seward, was in an adjoining room, and on hearing the noise in the hall opened the door, where he found Payne close up to it. As soon as the door was opened, he struck Robinson in the forehead with a knife, knocking him partially down, and pressed past him to the bed of Mr. Seward, where he leaned over it and struck him three times in the neck with his dagger.

Mr. Seward had been out riding shortly before the fatal day, and had been thrown from his carriage with great violence, breaking an arm and fracturing his jaw. The physician had fixed up a steel mask or frame to hold the broken bones in place while setting. The assassin's dagger cut his face from the right cheek down to the neck, and but for this steel bandage, which deflected two of the stabs, the assassin might have accomplished his purpose.

The carriage disaster was after this night almost considered a blessing in disguise. Frederick Seward suffered intensely from a fracture of the cranium. The nurse attempted to haul Payne off the bed, when he turned and attacked him the second time. During this scuffle Major Augustus H. Seward, son of Secretary Seward, entered the room and clinched Payne, and between the two they succeeded in getting him to the door, when he broke away and ran downstairs and outdoors.

The coloured doorkeeper ran after the police or guards when Frederick Seward was knocked down, and returned and reported that he saw the man riding a horse and followed him to I. Street, where he was lost sight of.

In some way Payne's horse got away from him, for a little after one o'clock on the morning of the 15th Lieutenant John F. Toffey, on going to the Lincoln Hospital, East Capitol and Fifteenth Streets, where he was on duty, found a dark bay horse, with saddle and bridle on, standing at Lincoln Branch Barracks. The horse no doubt came in on a sort of byroad that led to Camp Barry, which turned north from the Branch Barracks towards the Bladensburg road. The sweat pouring from the animal had made a regular puddle on the ground. A sentinel at the hospital had stopped the horse. Lieutenant Toffey and Captain Lansing, of the 13th New York Cavalry, took the horse to the headquarters of the picket at the Old Capitol Prison, and from there to General E. O. C. Ord's headquarters. After reaching there, they discovered that the horse was blind of one eye, which identified it as the one Booth purchased in November, 1864, from Squire George Gardiner.

Immediately upon the identification of Paine I arrested the Bransons and all the occupants of their fashionable boarding house, No. 16 North Eutaw Street. Following is a list of the persons arrested:

Mrs. M. A. Branson,	Mr. Chas. Ewart,
Miss M. A. Branson,	Mr. C. E. Barnett,
Miss Maggie Branson,	Mr. J. C. Hall,
Mrs. Early,	Mr. W. H. Ward,
Mrs. Croyean,	Mr. E. A. Willer,
Miss Croyean,	Mr. C. H. Croyean,
Mrs. Thomas Hall,	Mr. Aug. Thomas,
Miss Josephine Hall,	Mr. Winchester,
Mr. Joseph Branson, Jr.,	Mr. Thos. Hall,
Mr. C. H. Morgan,	Mr. S. T. Morgan,
Mr. C. S. Shriver,	Mr. H. D. Shriver.

I began my examination of the individuals in the house, seeking to find who, if any, were intimate with Paine, and might, therefore, have had some knowledge of the crime "before the fact."

Not all of these people were known to be disloyal. Messrs. C. H. Morgan, S. T. Morgan, C. S. Shriver and H. D. Shriver are marked on my list as "loyal," and there may have been others.

I have a lead pencil memorandum of the examination in the house (No. 16 North Eutaw Street) but it is so disjointed as to be unintelligible, and I will not put it in here. Finding that the most valuable source of information was the Bransons, I released all others, resuming the examination of Miss Maggie Branson in my office where I could be more deliberate.

Her statement is mixed and disjointed and there are repetitions. It took me much time to elicit the facts. She broke down and wanted me to destroy a great part of her statement and let her replace it with a truthful one, which I refused, requiring that all she had said should be put down.

Examination of Miss Maggie Branson.

I was at the General Hospital at Gettysburg about six weeks in 1863. I was there in the capacity of nurse. I don't know any of the surgeons except Dr. Simley, of Philadelphia, who would remember me. I went there to assist all the wounded soldiers. While there I saw a man known as Lewis Payne; he went by the name of "Doctor" and "Powell," he wore a pair of blue pants, I think, and a slouch hat; I did not have much talk with him while there.

I did not learn during the time I was there what he was. I don't remember of giving him my address. Sometime in the same year, after the above named occurrence, I saw him at our house; he called to see me. I can scarcely remember how he was dressed; but I think in a Federal uniform. I think he was stopping at Miller's Hotel.

He said he wanted to cross the lines but did not say where to, nor in what direction; he did not tell me where his home was; I don't remember what I replied.

I did not ask him anything about his intentions as to crossing the lines. I don't know that he told me what his intentions were; it was in the afternoon when he called. He again called at our house about the middle of January, 1865; he was dressed in black clothes; he said he was from Fauquier County, Virginia; he said he had just come in on the cars, and he wanted to board, but we could not at that time accommodate him; there was no one else present; he said he was a refugee and had his papers; he wanted to show them to me.

He said at Gettysburg that his name was Powell; on his second visit at the house he said his name was Payne.

At this point in the examination Miss Branson broke down. She realized that I was drawing her into a net of contradictions, and she thereafter proposed to be more frank and truthful with me.

He said his father was a Baptist clergyman; said he had two brothers that were killed in the army; it is my impression that they were in the Confederate Army.

He said a great deal of Mosby, and I should judge by his talk that he belonged to Mosby's Command. I have some slight recollection of his saying that he assisted in capturing a wagon train and some amount of newspapers on one occasion.

I have occasionally walked out with him. I called once or twice at Mrs. Heim, No. —— Race Street, with him, we saw Charles and William Heim there; he did not see Mr. Heim, he (Heim) was in Richmond; I never saw any one else there when I went with Mr. Payne. He told me that his proper name was Powell; he said this when he came here this year.

We also called on Mrs. Mantz, on Baltimore Street, near Green Street. I introduced him there as Mr. Payne. I might have called twice at this place. I often went to church with him. He was arrested at our house on March 12th, 1865, by Colonel Woolley's officers. I saw him after his release, on the day he was released; I have not seen him since. I heard from him only once, that was by a letter to my sister from New York.

I have sent provisions, &c., to prisoners of war at Fort McHenry and Johnson's Island. I consider myself loyal. I have a great many friends in the South, and many relatives. I have never taken the oath of allegiance.

"Mr. E. W. Blair used to meet Mr. Payne at the house very often. On one occasion he went with him to the theatre. Mr. Chas. G. Heim used to call on us and would see Mr. Payne.

If he had on a blue uniform when he came from Gettysburg, it was worn to aid him in getting South; it was not worn to act as a spy. I am confident that he never was North before. My sister said she thought at Gettysburg that he was a Federal doctor. Some called him Powell; I think he was introduced to me as Powell when he first came to our house. I think his correct name is Powell; he said his father was a Baptist minister, that he had lost two brothers in the war and that he did not know but that a third. His name may be Lewis Payne Powell. When he came to our house to board this year it was about the last days of January. Before coming there he boarded at Miller's Hotel about ten days. He called on us several times while he was boarding at Miller's Hotel. Sister or I entertained him when he came; his talk was principally of the ladies; he complained of his education.

After he came to our house to board I introduced him to the boarders as Mr. Payne. I said to Miss Hall, one of the boarders, that he (Payne) was from Frederick County, Md.

He was not particularly intimate with any one of the boarders. He was acquainted with all of them. My sister played chess with him; Mr. Barnett played with him. I have seen him speak to Mr. Joseph Thomas. I do not think they were intimate. I have spent considerable time with him. I think I spent more time with him than my sister or any of the other parties in the house. I walked with him very often. I was accompanied by Mr. Payne over in old town, on a matter of business, to employ some servants. I proposed to call on my cousin, Mrs. Dukehart, corner of Fayette and East Streets, and he agreed. I left him in the parlour alone, and went up stairs to see the family, and staid a short time and left. I am sure not a member of the family saw him; in the evening we called again. I called with him on Mrs. Heim on Paca Street, I might have called several times, we took tea there once; at other times only made short calls, at no time when we called was there any visitors there. Mr. Heim's business was in Richmond. Mr. Payne went to New York before Mr. Heim came home from Richmond. Mrs. Heim knew Mr. Payne was from Virginia. I don't know that she knew he was in the Rebel Army. I do not think Charles G. Heim was at any time home, when we called.

We (Mr. Payne and I) called on Mrs. Mentz, on Baltimore Street; she is my aunt. I think we called on her twice. She knew he was from Virginia. I don't know that my sister ever went out with Mr. Payne. I don't remember going to any other place except to church. I went several times; do not know exactly how many.

I remember his arrest on or about March 12, 1865, by Colonel Woolley. I came to this office and saw Lieut. Smith, about Mr. Paine. I thought he was arrested through malice on account of his whipping a coloured servant in our house; that was very saucy. I told Lieut. Smith that he (Paine) had not been North before since the war commenced. I at the same time knew he had; I did this to shield him from harm. After his release he came to our house and left almost immediately. My impression is that he went directly to New York.

After he arrived there he wrote me from the Revere House, directing me to address him at Revere House. I wrote him one letter; I addressed him as Lewis Payne. I never heard from him again, never saw him again after he left for New York; no one that I know saw him. I have always been a Rebel sympathizer. I have sent provisions, &c., to Confederate Prisoners at Forts McHenry and Delaware, Johnson's Island, Camp Chase, and Elmira, but only on permission of the military authorities.

When she had finished she was anxious to learn what I thought the Government would do to her. I informed her that she was responsible for Paine's acts; that if she had told me the truth when I had him in arrest, he would have been kept in arrest, and could not have attempted to assassinate Secretary Seward.

Miss Branson was detained a long time. Whenever you hear Paine spoken of in history as "Powell, the son of a Baptist minister" you will now recognize where the information came from.

The following from the New York *Tribune*, April 29th, 1865, describes one of those who had knowledge before the act. He had been intimate with Paine, and undoubtedly we were creeping up too dangerously near him. The suicide was buried in Greenmount Cemetery, and in the darkness of night we dug the body up as mentioned by the "Tribune." This was the only time I ever acted the part of a ghoul. If I remember right, the man was a builder and committed suicide out behind a barn in the country:

SUICIDE IN BALTIMORE.

A well known citizen of Baltimore committed suicide last Monday, a short distance from this city, by shooting himself with a pistol. No cause could be assigned for the rash act except that he had recently seemed depressed and melancholy. Subsequent events have induced the suspicion that he was someway implicated in the conspiracy, and last night the body was exhumed, embalmed, and sent to Washington, by orders of the Government. The affair causes much speculation, and there are many reports in connection with it as well as some facts which it is deemed imprudent to publish at present.

(*New York Tribune*, April 29, 1865.)

Paine was hanged, along with Mrs. Surratt, Herold and Atzerodt. Considerable silly sentiment was manufactured in Mrs. Surratt's case;

it was entirely wasted. If you will carefully examine her record you will say that her sex should not excuse such cold-blooded villainy. General Wallace was second in rank on the commission that tried the conspirators.

When President Lincoln's remains were lying in state in the rotunda of the Exchange in Baltimore, I remained at his head long hours, watching the faces of the people passing. Truly they were mourners, not the idle, curious, nor frivolous of mankind.

It had been intimated that the procession of people might be turned into a mockery. That mock ceremonies elsewhere would be attempted by some relentless furies. But even the suggestion was unhealthy. As a matter of history one of the earliest expressions of regret came from the Confederate prisoners of war confined at Point Lookout. Was ever man more universally loved?

Arrest of Mrs. Beverly Tucker

Richmond had fallen, Lee had surrendered and the end was near. Disbandment and readjustment, to a civil basis, was then in order. Whatever work I did after this was of that character. I was no longer to chase my dream of crippling Mosby. Probably he did not know I lived. He might have smiled at my proposition, but I enjoyed the dream nevertheless.

> Headquarters, Middle Department,
> 8th Army Corps.
> Office Provost Marshal,
> Baltimore, May 13, 1865.

Lieut. H. B. Smith.

Sir.—From what I can learn there are several gangs of counterfeiters of United States currency in this city, driving a good trade. I had the name and description of one of them but have lost it.

I now find that a certain John Mitchell (whom I know) engaged with a huxter in Washington, D. C., by name Henry High, knows all the particulars.

Mitchell will not come to this city as he is afraid of being arrested, upon what charge I do not know.

> Yours,
> Wm. L. Hopkins.

This was a new field for me and I delved into the matter with success. Counterfeit money, in slang, is called "queer," and those who pass it on the public are called "shovers." Its manufacturer never "shoves" it, but sells it in quantities to small shop keepers, car conductors, and others, at a certain percentage of its face value—50 *per cent.* quite usually;

the percentage, however, depends on whether it is well done or not.

Ramsey, at No. 146 Sixth Street, below Race Street, Philadelphia, was a medium. It was represented that the headquarters of the product was at Mahanoy City, Pa. I bought twenty-five dollars, face value, in twenty-five cent fractional currency very well done.

This was now a matter to be submitted to the Treasury Department, which I accordingly did, which was the reason for the following:

> Headquarters, Middle Department,
> 8th Army Corps.
> Office Provost Marshal,
> Baltimore, June 15, 1865.

Special Order No. 86.

1st Lieut. H. B. Smith, Assistant Provost Marshal, will immediately proceed to Washington, D. C., for the purpose of conferring with the Hon H. McCullogh, Secretary of the Treasury. On accomplishing the object of his visit, he will immediately report to these headquarters.

> By command of Major General Wallace.
> > John Woolley,
> > Lt. Col & Pro. Marshal.

Lieut. H. B. Smith,
    Asst. Provost Marshal.

> Headquarters, Middle Department,
> 8th Army Corps.
> Office Provost Marshal,
> Baltimore, May 25, 1865.
> 12 p. m.

Lt. H. B. Smith,
    Asst. Provost Marshal.

You will proceed to the Norfolk Boat, *Lary Line*, foot of Frederick Street, tomorrow morning, with a guard of one officer and twenty men, and carry out the instructions given you in compliance with orders of the Hon. Secretary of War.

> By command of Major General Wallace.
> > John Woolley,
> > Lt. Col. & Pro. Marshal.

The above was an interesting case. The party to be apprehended was a young officer, described as very youthful in appearance, who had shot and killed a private soldier under very aggravating circumstances. He ordered the soldier to do a menial service, and killed him for refusing.

The steamboat had three hundred or four hundred passengers. We did not want to delay innocent persons, so I allowed all to pass off who were of age sufficient to warrant the conclusion that they were not wanted. Then I searched the boat and found a mere boy who appeared to be not over fourteen years old; he was the one wanted. He had been tried and convicted, and was on his way to jail (I think the Albany penitentiary) when he escaped. We started him on again under a guard. When in the Thirtieth Street station of the Hudson River Railroad, in New York City, he was permitted to go into a water closet alone. He never came out the door. He must have crawled out through the window, though it seemed not large enough to permit even a boy's egress. The guards became frightened and deserted. No one ever heard of either prisoner or guards so far as I know. This boy officer was certainly living a charmed life.

Headquarters, Middle Department,
8th Army Corps.
Office Provost Marshal,
Baltimore, May 25, 1865.

Mrs. Beverly Tucker will be arrested. Seize and search her baggage for papers, and also cause strict examination to be made to discover any papers concealed on her person. Much depends on your diligence and skill in executing this order.

Watch carefully what companions she has, if any, male or female, and cause similar search to be made of such persons.

By command of Major General Wallace.

John Woolley,
Lt. Col. & Pro. Marshal.

To Lt. H. B. Smith,
Asst. Provost Marshal..

Camp Carroll Rioting

The muster out of troops and return to civil life of the men who had been hardened soldiers was attended with difficulties. The men often began to feel liberty while yet with arms in their hands, and rioting, the effect of too much "fire water" was frequent. Camp Carroll was a muster out rendezvous in the western end of Baltimore.

> Headquarters, Middle Department,
> 8th Army Corps.
> Baltimore, June 6, 1865.

Lieut. Smith:

I have sent four companies of infantry and a detachment of cavalry to report at Camp Carroll at once. They will be provided with ammunition. Find Colonel Johannes, 11th Md. Infantry, if you can, and direct him to take command of all reinforcements and enforce order in the Camp and neighbourhood; if Colonel Johannes is not there, see the senior colonel at the Camp and impart the order to him.

Brigadier General Lockwood has been ordered to proceed to Camp Carroll at once and take command.

Please report state of affairs from time to time.

> By command of Major General Wallace.
> Sam'l B. Lawrence,
> A. Adjutant General.

Headquarters, Middle Department,
8th Army Corps.
June 6, 1865.

Lt. Smith:

Send all the Cavalry you have to spare at once to report to the Commanding Officer, 11th Md. Infantry at Camp Carroll. Read the order I have written to him. Keep the three orders I wrote to General Lockwood and C. O. Federal Hill, and if you do not need them tonight, return them to me in the morning. Send the order at once to Commanding Officer, 11th Md. If anything serious occurs tonight send an orderly to me.

Yours, &c.,

Sam'l B. Lawrence,
A. Adjutant General.

Headquarters, Middle Department,
8th Army Corps.
Provost Marshal's Office.
Baltimore, June 6, 1865.

Colonel:

I have the honour to report in the case of the disturbance at and near Camp Carroll this evening.

I proceeded to the spot, assisted by Capt. Jones and Lt. Smyth with their commands. I arrested some forty of the ring-leaders. I then proceeded to the Camp to quiet the men.

I gave the Comdg. Officer of the 11th Md. a verbal order to place his men on guard over all of the troops not armed, and I promised him a written order from you, placing him properly in Command, in which case I herewith return you the orders given to Mr. Babcock.

After placing a guard over the Camp I had the country about patroled and all ordered in. Everything is now quiet. It had become a very serious matter and I felt justified in placing the 11th Md. on duty. Hoping my action in this case will meet your approval, I am,

Very respy. your obdt. servt,

H. B. Smith,
Lt. & Asst. Provost Marshal.

To Col. Lawrence,
A. A. G.

213

Lieut. Smith:

Your action is approved. I have no material present to write the order for Colonel Johannes, but will do so and send it to him.

Let me know where the Md. Brigade is, and if you apprehend danger or think the Brigade and the 11th Md. will fight if they are encamped together, let me know.

I send you the orders for General Lockwood and Federal Hill. If all is quiet, and likely to remain so, retain them, but if there is any indication of further trouble send them at once.

Please let me know where the Brigade is. I directed it to be encamped at Carroll, and cannot understand why it is not there.

Respectfully,

Sam'l B. Lawrence,

A. Adjutant General.

If the Brigade is at Carroll, the Commanding Officer should be directed to take command of all and use his troops. Let me know and I will give the orders.

The whole cause of the trouble, and reason why I know so little about it is that they were ordered to report to Colonel Brown, A. A. P. M. Gen'l.

I remained at the head of my department during all of 1865, and saw the veteran armies disbanded. It seemed strange to see the Confederates (Marylanders) who had been so long shooting at us, come home and resume their occupations at the desk or plow right before our eyes.

There were not many disturbances like the Camp Carroll riot. America may well be proud of the peaceable disbandment of the two great armies. There was no evidence of remaining venom between the fighters. Not so, however, with the slimy secret society disturbers who brought on the war, and nursed its continuance. Whenever a sneering, vitriolic sound is heard, you may be sure that it emanates from the copperhead element.

Indicted For Assault With Intent to Kill

June 25th, 1865, the Baltimore papers said:

Lieut. Smith, Wm. Earle, Kraft, and Babcock, of Colonel Woolley's office, were indicted for assault with intent to kill one
Jacob Ruppert.

General Wallace had always encouraged the civil authorities, so
that the establishment of martial law might be as little burdensome as
possible on the citizens. In this instance the fact of the military being
yet in control was overlooked. This Ruppert kept a low saloon on
"the Causeway," one of the hardest spots in Baltimore. I had sent for
him to report to me. He scorned the invitation; accordingly I went
to his place.

He blocked the doorway. I pulled him out, a scuffle ensued and he
bled some, but came away with me. His (Ruppert's) father had some
political influence from being able to control votes on "the Causeway"; he asked for an indictment. A warrant was issued from Judge H.
L. Bond (Judge Bond was a Union man).

Jake Dukehardt, a deputy sheriff, met me on Baltimore Street, and
informed me he held the warrant for my arrest. I assured him it would
be foolhardy to try to execute it, for one of us would certainly be injured. I recommended him to report to Judge Bond, and I assured him
I would be responsible for the results.

Judge Bond called on General Wallace, and explained how impossible it was to withdraw the order. General Wallace advised the judge
to use his own judgment, but telling him, at the same time: "If you
take Smith, I will place Alexander's Battery on the hill opposite the jail

and blow it down." This was the only clash between the military and civil authorities under General Wallace's administration.

FILE 45

Trip to Norfolk and Richmond

Headquarters, Middle Department,
8th Army Corps.
Office Provost Marshal,
Baltimore, July 5, 1865.

Special Order No. 93.

3. Lieut. H. B. Smith, Assistant Provost Marshal, 8th Army
Corps, will proceed to Norfolk, Va., with prisoners Manuel De-
sota and Morris Moran. On arrival he will deliver the prisoners to the Provost Marshal at Norfolk, taking receipt for same.
This duty performed, Lt. Smith will proceed to Richmond, Va.,
for the purpose of obtaining information in the case of Ralph
Abercrombie, after which he will return to these headquarters
without delay.

Quartermasters will furnish necessary transportation.

By command of Major General Wallace.

John Woolley,
Lt. Col. & Provost Marshal.

The above starts a train of reminiscences. Ralph Abercrombie, it
was alleged, had been used as a spy upon our men confined in Libby
Prison. He was confined with them, as though he were a prisoner
also, but it was his business to worm out the confidences naturally
confided to fellow prisoners, and to report them to the Confederate
authorities.

One of the purposes of my visit was to interview a lady residing
in Richmond who was a staunch friend of the Federal government,
and who had encouraged and aided our soldiers in confinement in
Libby prison and on Belle Island. Her name was Miss Elizabeth L.

Van Lew. She resided in a fine mansion on an eminence overlooking Richmond from the east.

I was greatly entertained by her stories of her experiences; she had come close to the danger line of confiscation of her property and her personal incarceration. She had at one time concealed in the cupola of her house, our soldiers, who had escaped from Libby prison, while Confederate officers were being entertained in her parlours.

I desired to learn if she recollected anything regarding Abercrombie's actions. As a recognition of Miss Van Lew's loyalty, President Grant made her postmistress of Richmond in 1869, which post she filled for eight years.

A few years after the war I gave a friend a letter of introduction to her, which she honoured. I was much pleased to be remembered by such a person. How such a kind hearted woman must have grieved, with a view constantly present from her home, of our suffering soldiers on desolate Belle Island!

Abercrombie was formerly a lieutenant in the 13th U. S. Infantry. He resigned in 1862 and went into the Confederacy through the blockade from Nassau. He was charged with having been the principal witness against Captain Dayton, who was executed at Castle Thunder, Richmond, on the charge of being a spy. He was arrested on the 18th of April, 1865.

Ordered to Philadelphia

The following is a copy of my release from duty to be mustered out:

Headquarters,
Middle Military Department.
Baltimore, July 19th, 1865.

Special Order No. 1.

1. Lieut. H. B. Smith, 5th N. Y. H. Artillery, is hereby relieved from duty as Assistant Provost Marshal, 8th Army Corps, and will rejoin his regiment without delay.

By command of Major General Hancock.

Adam E. King,
Asst. Adjutant General.

Official

(Signed)   Geo. H. Hooker,
Assistant Adjutant General.

Lt. H. B. Smith,
5th N. Y. H. Artillery, D. Co.

Headquarters, Middle Department,
8th Army Corps.
Baltimore, Md., July 20, 1865.

Lieutenant H. B. Smith, 5th New York Artillery, was on detached service as Assistant to the Provost Marshal, Middle Department, 8th Army Corps, at Baltimore, Maryland, during sixteen (16) months, 1864 and 1865, and always performed his duties zealously, efficiently, and promptly.

He won the confidence and esteem of the General Commanding, and all the officers of the Staff. As Lieut. Smith is to be mustered out of service, I take pleasure in thus furnishing him with evidence of the meritorious service he has rendered, and my belief that he will be equal to any trust that may be reposed on him, and entirely worthy the confidence of all with whom he may be associated in civil life.

Samuel B. Lawrence,
Lieut. Col. & A. A. G.

On August 1st, 1865, I was appointed as a civilian to perform the same duties:

Military
Headquarters, Middle Department,
Office Provost Marshal.
Baltimore, August 31, 1865.

Special Order No. 106.

1st. H. B. Smith, Commanding Detective Corps. Middle Military Division, will proceed to Philadelphia, Pa., for the purpose of obtaining information regarding a certain commissioned officer of the U. S. Vet. Res. Corps.

On completion of his duty he will report at these headquarters without delay.

Quartermaster's department will furnish transportation.

By command of Major General Humphreys.

John Woolley,
Lt. Col. & Pro. Mar. General.

Headquarters,
Middle Military Department,
Office Provost Marshal General,
Baltimore, Sept. 20, 1865.

Special Order No. 116.

2nd. H. B. Smith, Chief of Detective Corps, Middle Military Department, and one man as guard, will proceed to Washington, D. C., in charge of the following-named horse thieves: Michael Shea and H. J. Hoffman. On arrival he will deliver the prisoners with accompanying paper to Colonel T. Ingraham, Provost Marshal General, Defences of Potomac, receive receipt and report at these headquarters without delay.

Quartermaster's Department will furnish transportation.

By command of Major General Hancock.

John Woolley, Lt. Col. & Pro. Mar. Gen'l.

Horse stealing was much in fashion at this time.

Headquarters,
Middle Military Department,
Office Provost Marshal General,
Baltimore, Sept. 22, 1865.

Special Order No. 117.

2. H. B. Smith, Chief of Detective Corps, Middle Military Department, and one man as guard, will proceed to Washington, D. C., in charge of the following named horse thieves:

Wm. H. Smith and R. B. Franklin, alias Robert Nelson. On arrival he will deliver the prisoners with accompanying papers to Capt. Geo. B. Russell, Acting Provost Marshal General, Defences North of Potomac, receive receipt for same and report at these headquarters without delay.

Quartermaster's Department will furnish transportation.

By command of Major General Hancock.

John Woolley,
Lt. Col. & Provost Marshal General.

FILE 47

Captain Beckwith Convicted

Along about August and September, 1865, the Government ordered surveillance of all gambling houses, to discover if disbursing officers were gambling. This was my first experience in the art. It was a free school, for the tuition was on Uncle Sam. The lessons have served me all my life, and I have never wanted to go to that school since.

We appropriated from five to ten dollars an evening, to be spent in each house visited, depending on its standing. That gave us entry and made us welcome so that we could spend the evening. I gambled and observed, along with Captain Beckwith. I saw him win, and also saw him lose; lose far more than he could afford to. That was his undoing. Powerful interests were extended in his behalf and he was pardoned. Now read the two documents following:

> War Department,
> Adjutant General's Office.
> Washington, October 19, 1865.

General Court Martial.

Orders No. 584.

The action of Major General Hancock, Commanding the Middle Department, designating the Penitentiary at Albany, New York, as the place of confinement in the case of Captain D. L. Beckwith, 22nd Regiment Vet. Reserve Corps, Assistant Commissary of Musters, sentenced by a General Court Martial "to forfeit all pay that is now or may become due him to the date of promulgation of this sentence; to be cashiered and to be forever disqualified from holding any office of trust or emolument in the service of the United States, and to be confined for two years without pay, at hard labour at such penitentiary or

Military Post as the Commanding General of this Department may direct."

This sentence to be published as presented by the 85th Article of War, as promulgated in General Orders No. 23, dated Head-quarters Middle Military Department, Baltimore, Maryland, Oct. 10, 1865. Is approved. By order of the Secretary of War.

E. D. Townsend,
Assistant Adjutant General.

Official.

E. D. Townsend,

Assistant Adjutant General.

Headquarters,
Middle Military Department,
Office Provost Marshal General,
Baltimore, Oct. 29, 1865.

Special Order No. 127.

2. Special Officer, H. B. Smith, with one guard will proceed to Albany, New York, in charge of prisoner D. L. Beckwith. On arriving at Albany he will deliver the prisoner with accompanying papers to Amos Pillsbury, Superintendent of the Albany Penitentiary; receiving receipt he will report with the guard at these headquarters without delay.

Quartermaster's Department will furnish transportation.

By command of Major General Humphreys.

John Woolley,
Bvt. Brigadier General & Provost Marshal.

The "one guard" detailed to accompany me was General Woolley. He wanted a little rest and availed himself of this opportunity. Upon our arrival in Albany I hunted up my cousin, Edgar Jerome, who spent the evening with us at the Delevan House. We had a delightful evening listening to the General's stories. He was a charming story teller. Ed will remember especially his rendering of *The Arkansas Traveller*.

Now, Nettie, don't find fault with your history because your Uncle is not mentioned in its lines. In the histories of great events, such as our Civil War, it is an honour to be, even though hidden, "between the lines." Thousands who are mentioned in written history today will not be there when it becomes more ancient. Later on, when other great events crowd, only three names may remain. Lincoln, Grant, Lee. Perhaps still further on, only Lincoln, the martyr for liberty's sake, may be found.

Much of my work was between the lines of the two contestants, a more dangerous place than in the lines, for I was exposed to the bullets and sabres of both Southern and Northern Armies.

John H. Ing

We closed our headquarters in December, 1865, packing all records in finely arranged cabinets, which were then transferred to the War Department in Washington. When my relation with the government was terminated, through the instrumentality of General Woolley (Woolley had recently been brevetted), I was engaged by Mr. Archibald Sterling, an attorney (a prominent Union man), to go to southern Illinois to ravel out a contested will case. The contestants were a group of neighbours, headed by a shrewd woman.

If I remember right, under the Maryland laws, if a child died before maturity, there was no inheritance. Mr. Sterling claimed that the young man was not of age when he died, and that he died in 1835; but he had no evidence to prove it. He had only a death notice clipped from some paper with no date on it. But he had an anonymous letter signed: "Veritas," postmarked at Carlisle, Illinois, in which the writer, for a consideration, offered to put Sterling in possession of evidence that would defeat the claim; this letter was a few months old. Mr. Sterling could not comply. He could pay for no evidence without compromising his clients. With these facts only and equipped with the following letter of introduction, I started West:

> Headquarters,
> Middle Military Department,
> Office Provost Marshal General,
> Baltimore, Dec. 27, 1865.

Capt. Silas F. Miller,
    Burnet House,
        Cincinnati, Ohio.
My Dear Sir.——I shall be greatly obliged if you will make

Lieut. Smith, the bearer, acquainted with one or more of the conductors of the O. & M. R. R. Co.

Lieut. Smith is one of my officers, and comes west on business which takes him on the line of that road.

This is not for the purpose of securing a pass, but in order to get information. I have the honour to be,

Very Respectfully,

Your obedient servant,

John Woolley,

Bvt. Brigadier General U. S. Vols.

Provost Marshal General M. M. D.

The field was entirely new to me. All the way to Cincinnati and the rest of the way to Carlisle, Illinois, I put in much of my time in speculating as to the best course to adopt on landing in a small town, among a lot of villagers, who were banded together in this scheme. My name was to be Comings, and I came from New York; that was all settled in my mind; but what was my business there? I expected to be there a few days, and there was the rub; finally, after failing to fix up a story I concluded to "keep mum," entirely. Later you will see the fix which that conclusion came near leading me into.

I arrived there at night. I asked the landlord not to put me high up in the hotel, and he didn't; I learned the next morning that the hotel was only two stories high. I lounged about the tavern and the village two or three days, making myself aware of the surroundings. I tramped out to the fork of the Kaskaskia River, where the affidavits alleged the boy was buried in 1836. The river was a muddy little brook. No grave was to be found, but some little distance away was a burying ground. I went there searching for the grave. I found it not, but lying up against a fence was a headstone having the boy's name on it, and the date of his death.

In walking about the village I had many times passed the residence of the woman who had framed up the claim; she had noticed me. I wrote one of my old officers in Baltimore to wire me, in language about like this:

See Mrs. ——, confer fully and write me.

I instructed him to sign John H. Ing's name to it. Mr. Ing was this woman's attorney.

Equipped with this telegram I would be prepared to introduce myself to the woman as apparently having come there in the interest of Mr. Ing, her attorney, to look over the ground to see if matters alleged in the affidavits were susceptible of demonstration.

While waiting for the telegram I obtained the confidence of the postmaster. I impressed him that I was an agent of the Post Office Department, seeking to learn if he remembered a letter coming to his office addressed to "Veritas" (Sterling had replied to Veritas); he, having the too frequent curiosity of a village postmaster, said he remembered it well, and told me who the recipient was, and where he lived. He promised to keep secret my mission, and he did.

Mr. Truesdale, the proprietor of the tavern, kept horses, and I hired him to carry me to this man's house, quite a drive of three or four miles. On our way I found it desirable to seek his confidence too, and impress him I was an agent of the Post Office Department, etc. Mr. Truesdale seemed much relieved. He then told me he was so glad to know my true character. Being the only "unaccounted for" man in the village, I had been the object of suspicion, which, unrelieved, might have proven uncomfortable.

Carlisle was on the edge of the prairie. Live stock (marked) ran wild, until taken in; much had been stolen. A vigilance committee had been organized to punish the thieves. These people were about to conclude that the only "unaccounted for" man about was the "look out" for the thieves. Truesdale was wonderfully pleased to stand sponsor for me to them, without divulging my mission. Keeping perfectly mum came close to being poor judgment under these circumstances.

I saw Mr. "Veritas" and had a private talk with him. He promised to meet me in Carlisle the next day, which he did. Before communicating the information which he said he had, which comprised the name of the storekeeper who sold the material used for preparing the coffin in 1836, and who had books to sustain the statement, he demanded a promise in writing to pay him a large sum of money. Having a smattering of "legal lore" I drew up a bond to pay the required amount, in event of success. I kept a copy of the bond to show Mr. Sterling. It was signed by "George Comings." It was satisfactory to Mr. "Veritas," and he in an impressive manner wrote on a piece of paper, in large bold letters, the storekeeper's name: *Parmenus Bond.* We agreed to drive over to Mr. Parmenus Bond's place the next day, and we did.

I found Parmenus to be very old, over eighty. He confirmed the statement after he learned Mr. "Veritas's" greed had been satisfied. (I guess he was to divide with the old gentleman, in fact.)

Having disposed of this part I was ready to use the telegram I had received, meantime, upon the woman schemer. I called upon her, presenting my telegram from Ing. She was charmed to meet me, saying she had observed my presence about the village. I told her I had surveyed the ground pretty well. I asked her about the tombstone, where did she get it? She said she got it from Harrisburg, Pa. (about one thousand miles away), and would have it set up in the spring, I advised her that I concluded the evidence was presentable, provided her witnesses all stayed in line. She assured me that they would, as they all had a money interest in it, in the event of success. We then parted, and it did not take me long to get out of town. I went to St. Louis, thence to Baltimore.

When I arrived in Baltimore, I at once called on Mr. Sterling, but had to introduce myself, I was so unkempt, and my apparel so dirty. He was anxious to know my report; I told him I had the evidence but had to agree to pay for it. His face was a sight. He concluded I had ruined his case. I handed him the copy of my bond, "George Comings's" bond, assuring him that "Veritas" would have a difficult time finding the bondsman; that he would not want to find him until after success, that he would not speak of it in Carlisle, for his life. Mr. Sterling then laughed heartily. I made a full report, advised Mr. Sterling to call in Mr. Ing confidentially, and show him his fix. The claim was withdrawn, and "George Comings" was never called upon to settle.

The use by me of Colonel John H. Ing's name was not unwarranted. I had previously had a "run in" with him, which led me to believe that he was a criminal party in this scheme. At one time he was deprived of the right to practice before military tribunals in our Department, because of unprofessional actions. He appealed to General Wallace, who referred the matter to me to make an examination. Pending the examination a lunch was given at which Ing and I were present. I presume the lunch was to give Ing a chance to reach me.

He tried to, but the lunch did not answer its purpose. Upon my report he was practically disbarred from practice in military courts, based upon the evidence obtained. Therefore when I met his name in connection with this case I felt warranted in assuming he was the "promoter" of it. The use of his name was not forgery. He was deprived by it of nothing except, perhaps, an "unearned increment."

Governor Fenton's Letter

State of New York,
Executive Department,
Albany, 8th May, 1867.

Bvt. Major H. B. Smith.

Dear Sir.——I have the honour to transmit herewith a Brevet Commission, conferred by the President in recognition of your faithful and disinterested services in the late war.

In behalf of the State allow me to thank you for the gallantry and devotion which induced this conspicuous mention by the general government. I feel a lively solicitude in all that relates to the honour and prosperity of the Soldiers of the Union Army, and especially those from our own State, who advanced its renown while defending the cause of our common country.

Very Respectfully,

R. E. Fenton.

I believe there should be no continued ill feeling towards those who conscientiously bore arms against us. Nor towards their official spies. Nor towards persons who by reason of blood relationship or former close affiliations aided them. But towards those, who for personal profit aided them, and who sought to hamper us in our efforts to preserve the Union, we cannot cease to have contempt.

It is held that "everything is fair in war." If so, then the deceptions used in the secret service were fair. But the moral effect on the one who pursues such service is not pleasant. Such persons become so used to being impressed with possible dishonesty as to doubt mankind generally. I had to fight to overcome that tendency. It is a much happier condition of mind to be freer of suspicion. *No thing is stronger than it is in its weakest point* is an axiom. Almost every person has a weak point, which a detective seeks to find.

General Wallace's references to me were made after a period of forty years, during which time he had met me but twice. It was gratifying, greatly so, and I am perfectly willing to confess that I had "zeal," but prefer to let his opinion of my "ability" be passed upon by others.

I hope I have not injured the stories in their telling, but I am very afraid I have wearied you all.

New York, April, 1911.

Semi-Centennial of the Civil War.